१८

Curing Conflict

.

The Institute of Management (IM) is at the forefront of management development and best management practice. The Institute embraces all levels of management from students to chief executives. It provides a unique portfolio of services for all managers, enabling them to develop skills and achieve management excellence. If you would like to hear more about the benefits of membership, please write to Department P, Institute of Management, Cottingham Road, Corby NN17 1TT. This series is commissioned by the Institute of Management Foundation.

Curing Conflict

.

LESLIE P. LEWIS

the Institute
of Management
FOUNDATION
PITMAN
PUBLISHING

Pitman Publishing
128 Long Acre, London WC2E 9AN

A Division of Longman Group Limited

First published in Great Britain 1994

Consultant Editor: Simon Perry

A CIP catalogue record for this book can be obtained
from the British Library.

ISBN 0 273 60559 3

1 3 5 7 9 10 8 6 4 2

Photoset in Linotron Century Schoolbook by
Northern Phototypesetting Co. Ltd., Bolton
Printed and bound in Great Britain
by Bell and Bain Ltd., Glasgow

*The Publishers' policy is to use paper manufactured
from sustainable forests*

Contents

■

Facing up to friction

How friction leads to conflict

All conflicts start with friction, and it's at the friction stage that there's the best chance to do something about the root causes, before out-and-out war sets in. This is not to say that there should never be any friction – a company or organisation in which everyone goes smoothly along is probably not growing or changing, or facing up to new challenges.

Lots of things go wrong from day to day in the world of work, for lots of reasons. Problems can be caused by forces outside the company, cash-flow inadequacies, technical difficulties and uncountable other reasons. But healthy organisations can work out those problems and weather the storms if the people within the company are able to be flexible, creative, hard-working and, above all, to function as a team.

HUMAN RESOURCES

Generally, a company's most important assets are not machines, stock or buildings – they are almost always people. It is interesting that we are ever more sophisticated in the use of machinery, electronic-this and state-of-the-art-that, and yet we put so little time and effort into the use, understanding and maintenance of our most valuable equipment – ourselves. Office blocks are important, stationery is important, but we are slow and reluctant to take account of such questions as:

- whether people are fulfilled
- whether people are made to feel they belong
- whether people feel empowered
- whether people feel motivated
- whether people are encouraged to outperform themselves.

It is all these issues which cause friction, discontent, burnout, 'dis-stress' (ie. negative rather than positive stress), and lead to adversarial relationships within organisations.

WASTE AND LOSS

American research into management consultancy suggests that if your company is in a product business – say you make cups and saucers – you can expect to lose about 25 per cent of your gross turnover through waste, through error, machinery wearing out, replacement of moving parts and so on. In a service industry, the percentage goes up to nearly 50 per cent. And 85 per cent of that 50 per cent is lost through poor communication between people. That's how much is wasted. Note that there is a difference between 'waste' and 'loss'. A loss is much more identifiable – if you break something you can quantify what you have lost. But waste is very ambiguous, vague and amorphous.

The figures given above for waste may seem hard to believe, but let me tell you about a discussion I had with Charles, the chairman of a sizeable company with whom I was working as a consultant at the time:

Charles: Leslie, I find your waste figures hard to believe – and I'm sure our company is much less wasteful.

Leslie: Well, let me give you a real example. When was the last meeting you had?

Charles: I had one this morning.

Leslie: OK, tell me about it. First of all, who was there, and what was the point of the meeting?

Charles: The point was to get the 16 people on the executive board together to implement some changes in one guy's division. We last met two months ago, and he outlined the case and today we were just going to rubber stamp it, it was really already agreed. The meeting was to start at 9.30.

Leslie: What happened at the meeting?

Charles: We were all there by about 9.45. We chatted for a few minutes, and had tea and coffee, so about 10 o'clock we got under way. This guy stood up to make his presentation about 10.05 and talked for about 20 to 25 minutes. At the end of it, there were some polite questions but, in reality, he really didn't have all the information ready and he wasn't actually in a position to seek board approval. So we agreed to postpone it to another time.

Leslie: Then what happened?

Charles: Well, a couple of people had things to mention and we finished about 11.00.

Leslie: When did you first have a sense that he wasn't ready to ask for board approval?

Charles: After he'd been talking for 15 minutes or so, I started to think 'I'm not sure where we are going here.'

Leslie: Charles, you're hedging! When was the *first* time you had an inkling that this guy was not ready to deliver?

Charles: Well, to be honest, the moment I saw him. He seemed a bit nervous and, almost instinctively, I said to myself, 'He's not ready'.

Leslie: In retrospect what could you have done?

Charles: I could have telephoned him last week and said 'Look, we are really only getting together to approve your proposed changes – are you ready to make the presentation?'

Leslie: First of all Charles, you're the chairman of a large profitable company, and you're also very popular, so no one is likely to tell you, but what you did this morning was to waste two hours of company time, and I would like to put a figure on that. First we'll tot up all the attendance costs of the other 15 people on the board, plus the secretary, plus the coffee, plus the use of facilities – everything. What do you charge yourself out at? Your time has got to be worth £5000 to £10,000 a day, because one of your decisions could affect the entire company. You are extremely valuable. Adding you in, the total comes to almost £100,000!

Because you didn't say, 'Well if you're not ready, let's put the meeting off until you are, and if you can't sort this out in the time schedule you set yourself, you can't expect the board to waste time on it', you wasted £100,000. Today's waste will be replicated all the way down the line by people who are far less secure and confident than you are, and far more frightened of causing an upset. If you allow this culture to become established, mediocrity becomes the order of the day, and that's where the waste happens.

> That is my main thrust. I want to promote excellence in the field of interpersonal relationships in the business community. My system for doing this, which will be described and explained throughout this book, I've called 'Human Technology'.

HUMAN TECHNOLOGY: MANAGING AND MAINTAINING TO REDUCE FRICTION

I want to give all managers an idea of the workings of 'Human Technology', so that our capacity to get the best out of our 'human' tools (including ourselves) catches up with our skills in using computers, fax machines, and other high-tech equipment.

Einstein believed that we only use about 15 per cent of our capacities – I think that it would help us access the other 85 per cent or so if we learn to develop our instincts and our communication skills. Management by consistency, repetition and rote (largely left-brain functions) is too slow and inflexible for the dramatic period of evolution that the world is going through today. We need to learn to use and trust our right brain, which houses our instinctive and creative responses and reactions.

I think we should apply an understanding of Human Technology not just to companies and other business forms, but to any type of organisation, however large – whether it's the National Health Service, the police, or government itself. All these organisations should be open to improvement and development. Too many people take the running and operation of organisations for granted and even believe that in some way they run themselves. This is a mistake – organisations are hugely intricate and complicated structures, necessitating skill and ingenuity to run them; but they are like this because they are full of people with their own individual opinions and attitudes. When you put people into a situation in which they have to merge and blend their attitudes, judgements, opinions, expectations, fears and anxieties, the outcome – without Human Technology – can be chaos.

Chalkcheese Ltd – the scenario

Chalkcheese Ltd, established ten years ago, is a medium-sized food distributor to the UK domestic market. Last year it made pretax profits of £290,000 on turnover of £3.4 million. As well as distributing food via its depot system to wholesalers throughout the country, it also sells direct to the major supermarket chains.

Across the past three or four years the company has gradually introduced computers piecemeal throughout the office – the accounts department uses a customised software package, the marketing department holds mailing lists on an ancient database on obsolete personal computers, customer services work on powerful menu-driven machines and the rest of the company is littered with a variety of machines for word processing, producing reports, analysing data and so on. Everyone's complaining about the impossibility of transferring information from one department to the other, and the lack of access to data produced elsewhere in the company.

So, three months ago the Chalkcheese board of directors decided that the time had come to install an integrated network system, tying all the departments together. A 'think-tank' was selected of four people, one representing each of the main head office departments. Their brief was to work out exactly the company's needs, and their preliminary report and recommendations were due to be presented to the board six weeks after the group was set up.

But when six weeks had passed, no recommendations were forthcoming – the four people in the group were at loggerheads, their different departments closing ranks behind their representatives and rumours about rifts, rows and threats of resignations, firings and redundancies had been drifting about the office for weeks.

Recognising friction

Preventing and curing conflict starts with recognising signs of friction, diagnosing the causes of the friction, and then tackling them. First comes recognition, which it's tempting to put off until the problem has mushroomed and become entrenched. You're a busy manager, you have 'real productive work' to get on with. It's easy to ignore warnings of friction, particularly if you yourself are not someone who finds anger and confrontations easy to handle.

Management and maintenance of the 'human machinery' you work with and are responsible for, however, *is* your job, and you are not doing it properly if you ignore signs that things are going wrong.

DANGER SIGNS – OBVIOUS

- resignations
- sackings
- rows
- complaints from outside
- complaints from within.

Serious conflict doesn't occur instantly – it's always the result of a build up of friction over time, and may result from several causes. If you don't notice any signs until you start receiving resignations from key staff without warning, or walk in on out-and-out screaming rows, then you've left it very late, and drastic action must be taken. This would represent very much a 'fire-fighting' rather than a 'fire-prevention' management style.

Resignations

Staff may leave for lots of reasons, some of which may be beyond your control, such as the decision to move to another part of the country to be with a partner. But if good staff or managers leave giving any of the following reasons, there may be a serious problem:

- I just can't cope with the pressure of work.
- I don't think I'm getting the recognition and responsibility I deserve.
- I don't really enjoy working here.
- I don't get on with my workmates.

- I don't get on with my supervisor.
- No one in management has asked me about, or seems to care about, me or my career.
- I'm not paid what I deserve for the work I do.
- My staff give me no respect.
- I feel undermined.
- I can't see any prospect of personal or career growth.

Sackings

All supervisors and managers have to face up to the unpleasant task of dismissing an unsuitable employee from time to time. But when one department or one particular manager sacks staff frequently, or when someone you thought of as promising is sacked, it should be investigated. The manager may not understand what makes a team tick or may be out of sync with his team. An insecure manager who feels challenged by bright newcomers may seek excuses to get rid of them; overload them with work causing them to appear incompetent, or act so unpleasantly towards them that he inspires an insubordinate backlash of temper.

Rows

Not everyone is going to agree about everything, all of the time. There will be, and should be, disagreements about the way things are to be done, who should do them, how long things should take, how much things should cost and so on.

Professionals are paid to express their expert opinions, on the basis of their experience, judgement, intuition and skill. So you won't necessarily get the same opinion from two different experts. But there is the world of difference from two people enthusiastically defending some stance or suggestions they feel strongly about, in the full knowledge that they may have to reach an expedient compromise or that one may have to be prepared to back down and give the other her full support, and two people viciously attacking each other with irrelevant and often personal criticisms, and no intention of arriving at the best solution for the organisation, merely the intention to 'win' the argument.

Rows like this, with different sides taking entrenched positions, refusing to listen to each other's arguments or consider outside advice, are extremely difficult to resolve, and extremely damaging. It's rare that their effects are confined to only two people – others generally join in and take sides, and the row may spark off a whole succession of further arguments, which may mask the original cause or causes of the friction that led to the row. The row itself causes a rise in stress, anxiety and feelings of insecurity among other staff, particularly those who 'hate rows' or fear being sucked into the argument.

Complaints from outside

Complaints may come from outside the company about poor service, poor quality, poor response or many other things. Once the company or organisation has received a negative image in the eyes of the outside world, it is very difficult to regain confidence and respect. Conflicts within the company should be sorted out long before they reach the outside world.

Complaints from within

Most people want an easy life, and don't want to be seen as whiners or trouble-makers. Any complaint about a member of staff, a manager, or a department should always be investigated thoroughly. It is important to keep an open mind, however – someone who resents a superior or colleague may be trying to damage their reputation or get them into trouble, possibly to cover up some inadequacy of his own.

7

DANGER SIGNS – WARNINGS

There are any number of warnings of friction and potential conflict that an efficient manager should be alert to. A few examples are set out in Table 1.1.

DANGER SIGNS – SUBTLE HINTS

Finally, the very first signs of potential friction may be very minor indeed. As simple as noticing that while a certain group of people always go out to the pub together every Friday night after work, some people are never invited, or that people in one particular department are always out of the door like bullets from a gun on the first stroke of 5.00 pm. A few examples:

- reluctance to discuss group performance
- snide comments
- social divisions
- interdepartment competition
- clock-watching and poor timekeeping.

Chalkcheese Ltd – the players

Let's return to the company think-tank on new computer installation, introduced

Table 1.1

The warning sign	'Overheard'
Absenteeism	'Look at this report from personnel! Peggy's department has an average of ten days per person sick time, while the rest of the company has about three.'
Decisions not made	'Why haven't you ordered these materials yet?'
	'I passed the quotes to John three weeks ago, but he hasn't picked a supplier yet'
Decline in quality standards	'That's the fourth call this week complaining that the colour's not right in the last batch we sent out!'
Employees not reaching potential	'How's Fred getting on in your department? We were really sorry to lose him, but he deserved the promotion.' 'You could have him back as far as I'm concerned. He's not done anything very special since he moved.'
Errors are repeated	'Alice, you've made the same mistake in these statistics as you did last time!'
Errors can't be explained	'We've just had a delivery of specially printed leaflets. There are at least three times as many as we can possibly use, so most of them will be wasted.' 'How did that order get passed?' 'I don't know – no one seems to know where the order came from.'
Failure to follow instructions	'LPT's last order was filled and the goods shipped without anyone checking the current state of their account, although there was a memo from accounts saying that no orders over £1000 should go out without a credit check first.'

The warning sign	'Overheard'
Lack of creativity	'I asked for new ideas about how to proceed two months ago. We keep having these meetings, but no one's suggested anything.'
Meetings dominated by same person/group	'Susan always contributes a lot to the monthly meeting – the rest don't say much.'
Productivity drops	'How many finished projects has Ernie's department got through this year?' 'Forty.' 'That's strange – last year and the year before, they did sixty.'
Refusal to attend/arrange meetings	'There's a meeting on Tuesday about the new staff assessment system.' 'Look, I just can't spare time for that sort of thing, I'm too busy.'
Slow implementation of new initiatives	'How's your new quality control system going? Must have been in about three months now?' 'Oh, it's not really up and running yet – some parts of the system are having problems.'
Wasted management time	'Here's my report on information provision to the accounts department.' 'Didn't you know that accounts are being split into departmental sub-sections? Everything will be different in a month or so.' 'Oh no – it's taken me weeks to get this together!'

9

earlier in this chapter. The think-tank had spent six weeks getting nowhere, and now may be in a potentially deadlocked conflict situation. How did this come about? Could it have been averted if earlier signs of friction had been recognised and dealt with? First of all, who are the people who make up the think-tank?

■ **Stuart**, financial controller and head of the accounts department, who holds two briefs – to put the case for the accounts department's needs, and to allocate the necessary funds for whatever system the think-tank chooses.

- **Natalie**, a long-serving member of the customer services department, selected by her boss to work in the think-tank.
- **Patrick**, a relatively recent recruit to the marketing department who is full of new ideas and volunteered to be group representative.
- **Gail**, general office manager, with no particular title, but an unspoken responsibility for the smooth running of the office and integration of the different departments.

Act One

For the first meeting the group members were asked to prepare a short report on what computer systems each department were already using, and what for.

Let's follow the think-tank's deliberations as they happened. At the start of the meeting, Stuart, as the most senior in years and in position, clearly sees himself as 'chair' of the group, sits at the head of the table, and asks the others to present their reports. Patrick immediately butts in, saying 'There's no point in talking about what marketing have currently got – it's useless, and we need a complete change. I've got some ideas about what to do instead . . .' Stuart is annoyed at the interruption, and at the upset to his agenda calling for the collection of information from the other three in order to provide a starting point.

10

He cuts across Patrick, saying 'If you haven't prepared anything, how about the others – Gail?' Gail hands out a list of machines and software currently in use, and speaks for a few minutes about how the system is used. Stuart asks her why she hasn't mentioned the machines and systems used by personnel, to which she replies that she had not considered that part of her remit. Natalie then hands over a list of machines, but says that she can't really tell them anything more, as she doesn't understand how the systems function, only what she and her team do with them, and that the report was drawn up by her boss, who did not discuss it with her.

All four team members feel irritated and/or upset. Stuart is not respected by the other three, who think he's indecisive and a stick-in-the-mud. Patrick seems to be trying to take charge and is pushy. Gail prides herself on her professionalism, and feels it's been damaged through no fault of her own, and Natalie feels out of her depth.

. . . . **immediate result – friction; potential result – conflict.**

Friction and you

Where do you stand in relation to the signs of friction you've identified? A most important point to remember is that since friction can occur between any individuals, groups, or groups and individuals within the organisation, you are as likely to be part of the friction situation as anyone else. Ask yourself:

- Do I allow my personal insecurities, ambitions, prejudices or preferences to influence the way I make decisions, or communicate these to my colleagues and staff?

- Do I protect my position by keeping information and contacts to myself?

- Do I allow others to make errors through disinformation or lack of information?

- Do I support or collude in a 'them-and-us' relationship with other groups or departments within the organisation?

- What is my personal style? Am I, for example, open, closed, defensive, supportive, adversarial, autocratic, willing to make concessions and so forth?

- Does my style clash with that of the people I work with?

- If so, does it cause problems, or do the people around me understand my real meaning despite it?

- Am I unfair and unreasonable in my attitude to anyone I work with just because I don't like their personal style?

11

Action

A good exercise is to take some time to think about these questions, in relation to all the people you interact with frequently at work. You should write down on a piece of paper the names of individuals, groups and departments that you deal with, and next to them jot down, as fast as possible, your real feelings about each of them. It's worth repeating this from time to time.

Action

If you find yourself putting words like 'stupid', 'lazy', 'unreliable', 'prickly', 'aggressive', 'nice-but-dim' next to any of them, first ask yourself if these words are a true and fair reflection of the individual, or if they actually say more about your attitude to her. After all, if you repeat the exercise in three months' time, and still write 'stupid' and 'lazy' next to her name, and feel this is a fair assessment – what have you done about this, and, if nothing, why not?

Action

If you're considering a group or department, you should find yourself using a different sort of adjective, eg, 'productive', 'well-organised', 'efficient', 'obstructive', 'traditionalist'. Try and think about whether you are really *considering the group as a whole, or whether you are actually thinking about the individual you perceive as its leader or figurehead. If this is someone you find threatening, unpleasant or difficult to communicate with, you may be attributing your feelings about that individual to the group as a whole.*

Types and causes of friction

Sometimes it's hard to separate the signs of friction (arguments, avoidance of meetings, etc) from its causes. This is essential, because treating the symptoms is not going to deal with the root cause. I am sure that all friction arises from clashes both within and between individuals, and that these sorts of clashes can be categorised as follows:

- clashes of goals
- chain of command
- insecurity
- inadequacy
- personal style.

To me, friction is when one person rubs up against another, when there isn't mutual support in a team, when there isn't a natural accord. There are always different ways of doing even simple things – some people put the tea bag in the cup first, some people put the milk in the cup first: which is right and which is wrong? Both schools of tea-making are convinced they are correct, except those who are sure tea can only be made with leaves in a pot! In business, the important thing is the company procedure about making tea. But there has to be a determination that 'this is how we do things here'. The UK as a whole is a country of individuals, who are rather reluctant to say 'this is how we do things corporately'. In Japan, on the other hand, individuals desperately want to know, 'How does the company do things? What is the corporate policy on this idea?', and they welcome the clear targets that the answers provide. Here we don't, which is why we don't make good team players without conscious effort and hard work, and why there is always potential for friction.

An important element in Human Technology is the idea that individuals must feel fulfilled and satisfied by their job. I discuss some of the elements of personal needs and satisfaction in Chapter 2, but it's worth mentioning here that a key cause of friction is the 'square peg in the round hole' – the person who is, or thinks he is, in the wrong role for whatever reason. A crucial management function is to help empower people – help them to achieve their personal requirements within the bounds of their work role, and for the mutual benefit of the individual and the organisation.

> **There is a myth that it's OK to throw people into the deep end and see if they swim. It is very expensive because most people drown.**

There will always be a differential in empowerment between individuals, even those who have basically the same levels of skills and experience, if one is instinctively more powerful, more self-confident, more extrovert or more aggressive. In the move up the corporate ladder some will emerge as leaders, and will assume the mantle of power themselves, because it's in their nature. This may happen without being clearly formalised. These individuals act as leaders and are treated as leaders, but have never been appointed or named leaders, and their roles have not been established, formalised, acknowledged or communicated to colleagues. The others around them are not really clear about what responsibility either the 'leader' or themselves actually have. 'Does this self-styled *leader* have the right to tell me what to do? If I implement her decrees am I doing what the company expects or is she out on her own? Can I take this decision or must I refer it to the *leader*?' Friction arises from not being clear about who is supposed to do what and by when.

13

CLASHES OF GOALS

Goals are very largely what business is all about. An efficient company defines what end it wants to reach and when it wants to get there, and sets sub-goals as part of its chosen strategy for getting there. Routes that are seen as unproductive 'garden paths' are avoided, and hard decisions may be taken to forgo some tempting opportunity in order to concentrate attention and resources on what is seen as the primary goal.

Each department, partner, individual manager and member of staff should be clear about what the overall corporate goal is, and most importantly, what *their* goals are. In an ideal world these must be clearly defined by the board at the top level, and then split into sub-goals by supervisors at every level. If the company goal alters, or circumstances call for a change in strategy, the effect on sub-goals must be clarified, and passed on to the people who have to implement them.

If a company making widgets and thingummies decides to convert all its production to thingummies, it has to set new goals for:

- the widget salesmen: 'Push thingummies.'

- the materials buyers: 'Stop buying widget materials, and increase stocks of thingummy parts.'
- the training manager: 'Don't teach any new staff how to make widgets, and set up a retraining programme teaching existing widget-makers to make thingummies.' And so on.

The failure to reset any of these goals will result in friction. The failure to explain why these sub-goals are being altered in the light of changed corporate goals can be almost as damaging, giving wrong messages to managers and staff. For example, if the materials buyer is not told that the focus on thingummies is a long-term plan and the company never intends to make widgets again, he may not realise that he should be looking for good long-term supplies and keen prices for a period of time, rather than an immediate one-off purchase.

No clear corporate goals

Absence of decision making, or creativity and foresight at the highest levels of a company or organisation leads to a lack of motivation throughout the entire set-up. If the board does not, or cannot, agree on what to aim for, allows itself to be so caught up with the day-to-day running of the business that it avoids thinking about the future, then such a board provides no guidance to departments, managers or staff as to how to proceed. This is desperately frustrating for good managers – should they be developing or cutting back in particular areas? Can they invest in more staff? New technology? Should they be trying to attract in more business?

Start by laying down the *company* ground rules and goals, not any one individual's ground rules and goals. The more precise you can be about company rules, targets, and expectations, the easier it is to deliver a specific task or to achieve a specified goal.

No breakdown of corporate goals into department and individual goals

If corporate goals are set, it's equally important to think about the role of each part of the business in achieving the overall goal.

The board of Smith's Ltd decides to develop a computerised production process, gradually phasing out traditional methods of production. The goal is to make the new technological process account for half the group's revenue in five years' time. This is announced throughout the company, but the production manager feels completely at sea. There isn't room to start putting in the new computer technology unless he clears out some of the older machinery first. The old machines are busy – he'd have to turn away work. Has he authorisation to look for extra space temporarily? Has the board thought about this extra expense? All the current staff have their hands full running the current production. They can't spare time to retrain on the new equipment, but if new staff are hired to work on the new machines, what will happen to the current people when the old stuff is phased out? If they are afraid they'll be leaving together with the old machines, the work atmosphere of the next few years is unlikely to be pleasant and could be extremely unproductive.

Differing departmental goals

This can easily result from poor communication of the corporate goal to the rest of the company, or simply from allowing different managers and directors total freedom to interpret, or more likely *misinterpret*, the corporate goal in their own way.

15

If the production side of Smith's interprets the corporate goal to mean 'Replace old technology with new in five years' time', and sales takes it to mean 'Spend less time trying to find customers for the traditional methods and concentrate on drumming up clients who will use the high-tech methods', a serious and potentially disastrous conflict is on the way!

Differing personal and corporate goals

Personal goals are sometimes very hard to identify – even in oneself. Recognising a clash between an individual's life goals and those of the company can be very hard, but such a clash can give rise to friction.

Rose, the computer systems manager of Smith's, is very ambitious, and wants a seat on the board. At present, they make little use of computers, so her power and influence is relatively small. Implementing the new target will increase her status and responsibility enormously, and she's very keen that the initiative should be managed by her, and not given to someone from outside. She's actively pushing to bring in the new equipment as soon as possible, and dismisses as irrelevant the worries of the production manager.

CHAIN OF COMMAND

Any organisation consisting of two or more people will, from time to time experience conflicts caused by friction within the chain of command. There are several different sorts of problems that give rise to conflict:

- breakdowns
- blockages
- fragmentation
- grey areas of responsibility.

Chain of command friction usually arises because the employer has not defined the individual's roles and responsibilities clearly enough, nor established levels of responsibility – who reports to whom.

Breakdowns

Breakdowns occur when decisions are not made, are not clear, or are not communicated. Loops can be formed, in which one level refers decisions back to higher authorities for confirmation because of a lack of confidence in the immediate supervisor.

Blockages

Blockages can be caused by an individual who doesn't pass on information, either to senior managers, or to staff. He may disagree with a particular initiative or system he's being asked to work on, and be (consciously or unconsciously) trying to sabotage it. He may have a poor personal relationship with immediate colleagues so that information doesn't pass between them. Alternatively, knowing something that others do not may make him feel more powerful and important, and less inclined to pass on the information. Or he may simply be an unsatisfactory manager in that position; not aware of the importance of communication, or not prepared to spend time ensuring that staff know what they are supposed to be doing, and that his managers know what's being achieved in his department.

Fragmentation

This usually results from a personal conflict at a very senior level within a company or organisation, where departments, managers and staff take the 'side' of a particular individual. It's a risk where companies are spread out over different sites, particularly if these are distant, and the different groups have little contact with each other. Each group or 'following' develops it's own culture, values and targets, and a suspicious, competitive attitude towards the other group or groups. A charismatic director or manager will have a loyal group who are unlikely to question or challenge her decisions. In cases of conflict between 'their' leader and the board, or other group leaders, the team will back their leader up uncritically, even if she is acting as a maverick in this particular situation, and is out of step with the overall company policy or decision.

Grey areas of responsibility

A double-edged sword this, with problems arising in areas that more than one individual feels they have a responsibility for, and in areas for which no one takes responsibility. The grey areas of responsibility are often the weak links in the chain of command and the single biggest causes of friction. Indeed, one of the main advantages of total quality management (TQM) systems is that they require a detailed, comprehensive and clearly understandable definition of roles, responsibilities and accountability. Outside of TQM, it is very rare that precise roles and responsibilities are drawn up and very few people therefore know exactly what they are, and are not, responsible for. Accountability then descends into the gaps between who is and who is not responsible.

I had a client who owned several health food shops. He had heard an argument between two of his better employees. One was responsible for cosmetic products, and the other was responsible for the vitamins. Their roles seemed to be clear, and not to overlap. They were experienced, knew their own product lines and markets, and liked each other, and yet there was some friction.

The root of the argument was that in his design of the shops the vitamin shelves abutted the cosmetic shelves. They were both high-ticket items with good profit margins, so they both needed to be in prime areas of the stores. Each of the women assumed responsibility for setting up their products on the shelves. All the shelves were the same. One wanted to design her product layout one way and the other wanted to design her product layout a different way. There was no uniformity and they didn't look good together – it almost looked as if there was a separate boutique within the shop.

The vitamin manager thought that the cosmetic manager had very poor display skills, wasn't maximising the use of the prime shelf space, and was showing too few products. The cosmetics manager's plan was to show fewer products, but to allocate lots of space to each line, arranging them attractively, using a different stack layout for different types of product. She thought this allowed the customer to give more attention to the individual product lines, and prevented confusion and saturation by an over-abundance. The vitamin manager disagreed, saying that she should show as many products as possible, giving the customer a greater range to choose from.

They were both correct for the products they knew, based on their own experience. But who had the responsibility to decide between these opposing points of view? They agreed that the different layouts of the two parts of the prime shelf space looked wrong, but neither one of them had been given, or felt they could take, overall responsibility for shop design. Therefore, from the position of both employees, the position was insoluble.

INSECURITY

The manager who is insecure about his or her role within the organisation can lead to the kinds of problems described in the 'Chain of command' section above.

> **All conflicts you have with others must first be resolved within yourself.**

Insecurity can arise from:

- lack of experience
- lack of information
- lack of support
- lack of ambition
- lack of self-confidence.

In the chain of health food shops, the cosmetics and vitamins managers really needed someone to adjudicate between them. The problem was that the owner of the chain had not made a decision on layout for the prime shelf positions. He had never had a retail outlet before and he didn't realise this was an important policy issue.

Because he lacked retail experience, he didn't make a decision, and instead told the managers to sort it out between themselves. But the situation was a real impasse, with both managers' positions becoming more and more entrenched over time. What had been a good working relationship between the two women became damaged, and more and more breaches began to appear between them. Other staff, all of whom were unsettled by this disagreement, were taking sides with one manager or the other, unable to get on with their own shelf-stocking. They wasted time as they debated with each other about what to do, what the answer was, what the owner wanted, what would happen next, and the implications for their own jobs and positions.

INADEQUACY

We've all experienced cases of individuals ending up in management and decision-making positions which they are simply unsuitable to fill. One of the main tasks of Human Technology is to recognise that different people have different levels of creativity, leadership ability, organisational ability and communication skills – and that some people, who may be great at *doing* a job, are not right when it comes to managing others in the same job.

Another point about Human Technology is that we need to move away from the value system which awards much higher status to certain sorts of skills, forcing people to move away from roles in which they are happy achieving fulfilment from doing their jobs well and maximally, and into 'supervisory' roles instead. Their self-esteem may be satisfied by the job title, but they may also feel deeply insecure in the knowledge that they don't perform well in the role, they lose the enjoyment gained from completing a project successfully, and feel vulnerable to challenges.

The inadequate manager is the man who won't pass on full information to his staff, in order to keep one jump ahead. Who will take credit for work done by others in his department. Who'll contribute little or nothing to meetings with colleagues for fear of looking foolish. Who won't appoint new employees who might try and dethrone him. If he has other skills and abilities that the company needs, something must be worked out to allow those to be utilised and to recognise his value to the company, satisfying his need for status, without forcing him into a role he can't fill.

19

Different levels of task achievement

Clearly, an employee who is not competent to do her job, should not be doing it. But what should be done about the differential between people who do all that is asked of them, and no more, and those who give 105 per cent all the time? This is where the corporate culture is important. Is it OK to be mediocre? Or will the mediocre be weeded out, rewarded less or sidelined? Those giving 105 per cent will resent being treated the same way as those who coast. They'll feel the others are not pulling their weight, and that management is allowing them to get away with it. This will cause bad feeling and friction, with the high achiever complaining, openly or privately, about the other's laziness and lack of commitment.

A key aspect of task achievement for leaders (at whatever level) concerns willingness to solve problems. It is easy to point out what doesn't work, but much more difficult to provide and implement solutions.

As well as complaining, a high achiever has other options – to stop giving of her best or to leave. Both of these are wasteful for the company, and must be prevented. If the company can't make some sort of public distinction between the high and low achiever (additional rewards for the high achiever, penalties for the lower achiever for example), then it is better for the company to get rid of the low achiever than to risk losing the better employee. Some ideas about motivation, rewards and punishments are discussed in Chapter 2 and in Chapter 9.

PERSONAL STYLE

Last, but not least, of the types and causes of friction I'm going to discuss here, is personal style. This is the outward expression of our personality, and often the first thing that comes to mind when we are asked to describe someone, even in a work context:

- *'He's easy to get on with – always listens to the other point of view.'*
- *'You can rely on Pat, she's always the same.'*
- *'John gets irritated so easily.'*
- *'She's so arrogant.'*

If Jim always rushes into each new project full of optimism and enthusiasm, and Jane always takes the pessimistic and cautious approach, checking and double checking, they're sure to rub each other up the wrong way. He thinks she's a boring stick-in-the mud, she thinks he's a flighty boy-racer and not serious enough. You'll never change them – that's how they are, but you might change their attitudes to each other.

Can you get Jane and Jim to respect each other's skills, abilities and experience, and to recognise that as a team, they could complement each other perfectly? Get them to discuss their histories, their successes and their failures. If Jim can see that from time to time his enthusiasm has blinded him to pitfalls which he could have avoided, and that Jane's caution has sometimes paid dividends then he'll be able to accept that it's worth considering her concerns when she expresses them. At the same time, Jane must accept that Jim's instincts can be good and that his enthusiasm can help motivate others, and admit that over-caution can cause missed opportunities.

Action

Think about your personal style and that of each of your colleagues. How does each of you fit into the following:

- *Active or passive?*
- *Introvert or extrovert?*

- *High-flyer or plodder?*

- *Traditionalist or innovator?*

- *Eccentric or middle-of-the-roader?*

- *Cautious or risk-taker?*

- *Optimist or pessimist?*

- *Saver or spender?*

- *Thinker or doer?*

There's more in Chapter 4 about planning a profile of yourself and your co-workers, but thinking about your responses to the above lists should give you some insights into friction situations you've encountered.

FACING UP TO FRICTION – A CHECKLIST

- All conflict starts with friction. Curing conflict should start at the friction stage.

21

- Friction and conflict cause waste.

- The most important asset a company has is its people.

- Understanding, managing and maintaining a company's 'Human Technology' is vital to it's success.

- People who feel insecure, confused, overstretched or undermined can cause friction.

- You yourself may be a cause of friction – the greatest knowledge is self-knowledge.

- Every company should set and communicate clear goals, both for the company as a whole, and for individual departments, managers and staff.

Understanding what makes people tick

G etting to grips with people (Human Technology) is all about under-standing what makes them tick. What makes them do and say what they do? Why does one person react well in the face of a challenge while another goes to pieces and panics? Can you predict the behaviour of any given individual?

Chalkcheese Ltd – inside the players

During the first think-tank meeting (see Chapter 1, p.10), Patrick suggests that this is a great opportunity for a complete revamp of the way the administration of Chalkcheese operates. He talks with great enthusiasm about his 'vision of a completely new way of doing things'; 'integrating all departmental work'; and 'getting rid of outdated and unnecessary routine jobs'. Gail questions Patrick about the precise changes and new initiatives he has in mind, but he's pretty vague about details. Natalie likes Patrick, who's an enthusiastic and persuasive speaker, and overtly supports his suggestions, although she is very reluctant to put forward ideas and opinions herself. Stuart is infuriated by Patrick. He repeatedly tries to shut him up, and to return to the original agenda. He accuses Patrick of trying to get out of doing any work that he (Patrick) considers boring. He clearly thinks Natalie is negligible, and cuts across Gail's attempts to put Patrick's ideas into workable order.

This is what the players think about the meeting and their behaviour and feelings during it.

Patrick: I really can't see the point of going over old ground – I want to make a dramatic leap into a whole new sort of organisational system. I'm not going to waste my time writing reports. Stuart is just past it – he's an old fogey and wouldn't recognise a good idea if it bit him. Gail is obsessed with rules and procedures, and Natalie doesn't really know or want to know anything outside her own department.

Natalie: I really hate the atmosphere of this meeting. I don't see why everyone has to be so combative. I like Patrick, and think he has good ideas, although I can't really see how I fit in with them. I feel sorry for Stuart, because I don't think he knows much about computers, but I don't see why he has to be so dogmatic.

Stuart: I'm fed up with all this pie-in-the-sky impractical nonsense that Patrick keeps talking about. I want to get on with the job in hand – picking a new system so that we can do what we do more efficiently. He just doesn't know his place – he's young and new to the firm. He should keep quiet and learn from those who know better. He has no respect for age, experience or tradition!

Gail: I can see that Patrick has the germ of a good idea, but I'm sure he'll never work out all the details of it. I agree that this is the chance to do some major restructuring, and think we should take it – but I want to look at all the options first. None of the others is going to take control of this, so it's a good chance for me to really do something major. It could make a big difference to my position within the company, and will look good on my CV.

Why do we do what we do?

In this chapter, I want to talk about some of the things that make up an individual's behaviour patterns, and that form the foundations for my Human Technology system. Things like inherited instincts, culture and tradition, childhood experiences, and social rules. I want to look at what makes people behave 'out of character', and at how tension and friction within an individual can cause friction with others and conflict within the organisation.

When dealing with teams, groups and departments, it's easy to forget that they are made up of very different individuals, and that each person consists of more than just the attributes that fill a job description. It is sometimes more important, and of greater value, to have a group of people who get on with each other and where the team requirements take precedence over 'stars' whose egos or technical brilliance get in the way of the team.

In trying to answer the question 'What is personality?', key areas examined in this chapter include:

- the past
- the unconscious
- defence mechanisms
- human needs and motivation
- rewards and punishment.

When thinking about how people behave and why they behave the way they do, a good starting point is to remember that the greatest form of knowledge is self-knowledge. Why do *you* behave in certain ways in certain situations? What are *you* capable of ? How will *you* react under pressure? Or under attack? This is the first place to start when considering interactions between people, because it leads to so many valuable discoveries:

- self-awareness
- self-acceptance
- self-belief
- self-confidence
- self-esteem
- self-respect
- self-love.

Once we start to work out what makes *us* tick, we can suddenly find that other people are less unsettling, that we do not feel under attack and can therefore be less defensive. We inevitably become more self-aware, more at ease with ourselves, and therefore less threatened. It is a short step from becoming more at ease with ourselves to becoming more at ease with others. In any team situation – whether in business, or in social, sporting or family activities – being more at ease with others means we more readily accept their strengths and shortcomings and quickly learn to develop more realistic expectations of what the team can, and cannot, do. In the business context this means fewer adversarial expectations and more commitment, more efficiency, less waste of human resource potential and increased productivity. Without knowing and understanding each other's behavioural patterns, an individual's performance, productivity and effectiveness can be frustrating to management, subordinates and to fellow team members.

In the day-to-day hurly-burly of business, managers and team members don't usually have the skills, training, time or need to do in-depth personality analyses of themselves, staff and colleagues. But they would be short-sighted if they failed to consider the different behaviour patterns of the people they work with, and the interactions between them. These can be even more important – and potentially damaging – than what sort of qualifications or training an individual may bring to the job. In creating a high-energy team, I often find it more valuable to bring together a group of people who like, respect and enjoy meeting with each other and, in this regard, the traditional CV has little value. The cleverest people are so often liable to create a moat around themselves by being disdainful, arrogant or snobbish.

This book introduces a 'user-friendly' way of looking at individuals – including yourself – in a business context. The system aims to help predict how people will react in different situations, how they will interact with others, how to get the best out of people, and, most importantly, how to use what you know about individuals to prevent and cure conflict.

Generals, Nurses, Performers and Soldiers

The Human Technology system divides individuals into four 'character' categories dependent on their dominant personality traits. The character groups are labelled: Generals, Nurses, Performers and Soldiers. These group names don't reflect anything about the actual jobs of the people concerned, they are not intended to imply a hierarchy, and each is of equal value and importance to the team.

I came up with these character labels after some time spent helping business sort out conflict situations caused by clashes between people. Some of the scenarios I saw made me think of a war going on, with Generals directing the action, Soldiers doing the fighting, and Nurses caring for the wounded. In the middle of it all you get the Performer – the entertainer who comes along and puts on a show, which can be appropriate when the troops are not actively engaged, and a completely unhelpful distraction when shells are flying all over the place and everyone's attention is elsewhere. Performers can play any sort of role, they have complete flexibility. The other types show a certain sort of fixity.

Briefly, the four types in the Human Technology system are:

- **Generals**: Analytical and authoritative; organised and orderly; manipulative; can be good team leaders; good communicators.
- **Nurses**: Supportive and intuitive; easily wounded; can be willing to give their all; defensive if attacked; hate confrontation; rarely feel in control.
- **Performers**: Inspirational and innovative; not team player; entrepreneurial; like change, action, movement, 'fireworks'; hate rules, regulations and discussion; need guiding.
- **Soldiers**: Practical and hard-working; loyal; uninnovative; need directing; unhappy with change; willing to give their all; solid and consistent.

One of these four characters dominates the personality of each of us and, put simply, represents a measure of an individual's reaction to any given circumstance. For example, if you are rude to Performers their reaction is likely to be almost unnoticeable – it's like water off a duck's back, and will have been forgotten within seconds. Generals react differently: their first instinct will be to analyse what is happening; 'Let me think about that,' they will say. 'Why is this person being rude to me?' If you are rude to a Soldier the response will not be remotely analytical – you are likely to be punched on the nose. Similarly, no thought will precede a Nurse's spontaneous reaction, which, due to feeling so hurt, will be to burst into tears.

The different reactions have nothing to do with what sex you are, your background, education, age, and so on – they are personality-dictated, instinctive responses to a given situation. Understanding them pays enormous dividends.

As well as this dominant signature of the personality of each of us, we are, in addition, 'controlled' to a lesser degree by another of the four characters – the minor or secondary component of our personality. There are people who are almost exclusively dominated by one element: Lady Thatcher, for example, is about 90 per cent General and 10 per cent Nurse. She is predominantly autocratic, organised and analytical, with just a little of the intuitive, emotional properties associated with Nurses. More often, however, the balance between major and minor components is less clear-cut and we need to ascribe careful weightings to each. This can become especially relevant as the balance between characters begins to change during the middle years of our lives – a subject examined in Chapter 3.

You'll find a fuller description of the four different characters in the behaviourial system in Chapter 3, and in Chapter 4 some techniques for identifying characteristics in yourself and others. But first let's look at some of the underlying causes of behaviour, and identify some of the components that make up a person's 'personality'.

Chalkcheese Ltd – how the players fit the Human Technology system

The four players in the Chalkcheese think-tank are examples of the four types in the Human Technology system, and we'll use their discussions, progress, and lack of progress as examples throughout this book.

The dominant signature of the personalities of each of the players is:

Gail: **G**eneral
Natalie: **N**urse
Patrick: **P**erformer
Stuart: **S**oldier

What is 'personality'?

There are umpteen different ways in which researchers have tried to explain and define differences in personality, many of which have become embedded in popular culture. Some of the words and ideas they've used are familiar to us as part of 'common knowledge' even though we don't think of these ideas as being 'personality theories'. Concepts such as 'ego', 'motivation', 'pessimism' and 'repression' are part of everyday language, but what do they really mean? And how can you use such concepts to help understand the actions of the individuals and groups you work with – and, in particular, how such concepts become causes of conflict?

THE PAST AND THE UNCONSCIOUS

Adult behaviour is a composite of instinctive behaviour based on unconscious, inherited drives, social and cultural rules and ideas of what's 'right' and 'best', and actual life experiences. In any situation all three of these elements may be pulling in different directions, causing the individual stress and tension. Here is an example from a departmental head at one company I worked with:

27

'When I have to reprimand a member of my staff for poor quality work or bad timekeeping, I get really tense. I feel I just want to ignore the whole situation, not risk making them angry and shouting at me, but it's part of my job to make sure that those who work in my department obey the rules, and I wouldn't be doing my job properly if I didn't. In the past I've found that if I get into confrontational situations with people they easily bully me into not saying everything I should, or not making them change their behaviour even if I know I'm right. I've usually ended up apologising to them! So I tend to put these things off until they do something so bad that I **have** to speak to them about it. Then I feel really angry that they've put me in this awful position. Sometimes that means that instead of clearly explaining what they've done wrong and telling them what I want them to do about the shortcomings, I start shouting angrily at them, which I don't think is good behaviour for a manager. All that really happens then is that they hear and receive the anger and miss the information I'm trying to impart.'

In the Human Technology system, the Generals do a good job of balancing the inputs from the instinctive and the rule-based sides of their personalities. They are very logical and more likely to weigh up options than to dash off, following their instincts. Performers are very instinctive, and often can't explain why they want to do something – they just 'know' it's right. Soldiers, on the other hand, prefer life to run according to rules. They find it hard to cope with people who don't seem to live by the same set of 'life guidelines' as they do, and are most likely to reject any ideas which deviate from their rules as 'wrong'.

The instinctive part of our personality is not rational, and has no sense of time, and doesn't change with experience. It's behind our impulsive 'out-of-character' actions and speech, and pops up out of the blue or in our night-time dreams. That's what's working when we hear words popping out of our mouths over which we seem to have no control. I believe that only our instinct is right, and what often tends to happen is that our emotions at best dilute and at worst drown out the instinctive part of our personalities.

> **The head may mislead but the heart never lies.**

The social part of our personality contains a whole set of rules and standards that reflect the input of parents, teachers, and other authority figures. Even when a person believes themselves to have moved away from the rules and standards of their upbringing, they may suddenly find themselves experiencing intense guilt or embarrassment when their 'conscience' reminds them that some current behaviour does not conform to deeply engrained rules of behaviour. This can cause deep internal conflicts within an individual, which can spill out into workplace conflicts. Since these dictates are largely unconscious it is also hard for people to realise that their own 'rules and standards of behaviour' may not be the same as those of others – partly because they may not fully recognise them themselves.

The logical, problem-solving, conscious part of our personality has the job of bringing these disparate driving forces together, and trying to satisfy the demands of both, while still operating within the real world. This is why we suffer from anxiety when unable to resolve conflicts between desires and actuality, and why we use all sorts of defence mechanisms to protect ourselves from damage. These include a variety of serious-sounding ideas, such as projection, denial, displacement, rationalisation and repression, but in essence they're all very straight-forward.

EXAMPLES OF DEFENCE MECHANISMS

Table 2.1 contains some practical instances of defence mechanisms that may be operating in a given situation. Any of these explanations *could* be true, but they could also conceal some other reason for Fred's reluctance to visit Jones Ltd, which he's unwilling to admit, even to himself. You'll have to help him examine the reality of what he's telling you, in order to reveal the truth – to both of you! For example, you might

Table 2.1

Your department has fallen behind its sales targets, and on checking the records you notice that Fred, your lead salesman, has done fewer trips than usual recently, and that no one has visited Jim Brown of Jones Ltd, one of your best customers, in two months, and their purchases are down. You ask Fred for the reason:	
Fred's explanation	*What could be going on*
'Oh, haven't I been out as much recently? I didn't realise – I'm not sure I've been noting all my visits down'	Repression – unconsciously refusing to deal with, or remember, things that cause anxiety.
'Last time I went to Jones Ltd, I got the feeling that Jim thought I was calling too often, and didn't want to see me so frequently.'	Projection – attributing the cause of one's behaviour to some other person or reason.
'I've been on the road as much as ever, and visited Jones Ltd as often as usual!'	Denial – refusing to admit what is happening.
'I've been busy reorganising the customer files and planning new routes.'	Displacement – doing and thinking about anything other than the source of anxiety.
'Fewer visits is not the reason for sales drop-off – Jones Ltd is moving into different areas and don't need as much from us any more.'	Rationalisation – inventing and believing reasons for the situation other than the anxiety-producing reason.

29

discover that Fred had a really nasty near miss on the road to Jones Ltd on his last sales trip, and has been feeling very anxious about driving ever since.

Repression

Unconsciously refusing to deal with, or remember, things that make us unhappy or create a state of tension is quite common in work situations. For example, a member of staff who repeatedly forgets to do something may be subconsciously avoiding that job because they dislike doing it, or are afraid of failure. Trying to deal with cases of repression can be difficult, because just as the person wants to avoid *doing* the stressful task they will also want to avoid *talking* about it, to avoid the stress that

that will cause. If you force them to confront the repressive behaviour they may feel guilty and angry, and will resent your 'interference'.

Projection

Attributing the cause of your behaviour to some other person or some other reason. Fred really believes that Jim doesn't want to see him, because that's much easier to cope with than the frightening thought that he might not be able to drive any more, putting his livelihood at risk.

Denial

Not allowing oneself to believe what is actually happening. Even confronted with his job sheets and mileage records, Fred will continue to swear angrily that black is white, and that he is actually making as many trips as before.

Displacement

Doing other things to prevent oneself from having to tackle or face the source of anxiety. 'Busy' work can convince both Fred and everyone around him – for a while – that he's up to his ears in office tasks. Only later will it emerge that he's not been performing his major task, and instead has been doing lower priority work, or things that could be done by others.

Rationalisation

Giving oneself reasons other than the real ones for avoiding the anxiety-producing situation, or for the alteration in behaviour. Even if Fred is caught out – if you discover that Jones Ltd are buying the same products that you used to sell them from another supplier – he may continue to extend his rationalisation further and further until it becomes ludicrously transparent, rather than admit to himself the real reasons for stopping the visits.

The important thing to remember about all these defence mechanisms is that the person using them is not aware that he is doing so. If you 'catch him out' and face him with the difference between actuality and the reality he's constructed for himself, the underlying tension will be increased even further. You have to decide how important it is to sort out this problem. Is it worth making someone face up to and deal with whatever their real problem is? Or can the job be rearranged so that someone else takes on that role?

Chalkcheese Ltd – Stuart's predicament

Stuart is someone who has moved up with his job, but only by being in it. He has never created anything new and is now feeling worried that a leadership role is expected from him that he doesn't feel comfortable with – he'd rather have someone tell him what to do. On the other hand, he also thinks his seniority and experience has earned him the right to some status and respect. He feels threatened by the younger, more charismatic Patrick, who seems able to spin off an idea every time he opens his mouth, but whom he doesn't trust, and thinks of as a butterfly. Rather than admit his vulnerabilities, inadequacies and fears, Stuart blusters and tries to shout Patrick down – feeling as if he should be out to take control of the think-tank, although knowing in his heart that he would feel uncomfortable in the role.

SATISFACTION AND BOREDOM

Some approaches to understanding what makes people tick are based on the idea that all human behaviour results from attempts to reduce tension (unpleasantness) and to increase pleasure. This suggests that people who take great pleasure in their work, and find it satisfying, have had the good luck to find an occupation which allows them to realise some of the drives and work out some of the repressions experienced in childhood, in a socially acceptable and rewarding way. Otherwise, why would people who have no need to work for financial gain continue to do so?

Boredom can be thought of as a state of considerable psychological tension, which must be relieved by action which the person finds exciting and stimulating. Boredom can lead to dangerous impulses to remove the boredom, and a bored individual may be tempted to do something destructive or damaging just to break the boredom cycle.

In the Human Technology system, Performers, because they always need change and something new, are easily bored, and will do anything to avoid this state. Soldiers, because they feel at home with repetition and a sense of continuity, find it much easier to cope with boredom: as long as they feel they are following their intended path, and nothing happens to throw them off balance, they will continue, even if it means repeating a procedure or situation again and again.

Nurses gain most of their satisfaction from creating and maintaining a warm, supportive, loving atmosphere. If they can enable a loved one to achieve their targets, that too is very satisfying, particularly if their support is recognised and the loved one is grateful. It's not that they get vicarious pleasure from the other's success – it is their own success in the support role which rewards them.

Action

Some questions to ask yourself:

- *Which particular parts of my daily work do I find satisfying?*
- *Why?*
- *Are there other parts of my work which I could make more like the parts I enjoy?*
- *Which jobs do I not enjoy?*
- *Why?*
- *Do I do the jobs I don't enjoy adequately?*
- *Could I do them better by reorganising my approach to them?*
- *If not, would it make more sense to delegate those jobs to someone who would find them rewarding, and would therefore do them better?*
- *Am I reluctant to delegate or hand over tasks that I don't enjoy or don't feel I do well because I think that my responsibility for them adds to my status? That being entrusted with them is a mark of my position in the company? That people will think I'm lazy if I rearrange my work so that I don't do them any more?*

Centred and uncentred

A useful evaluative concept is that of being 'centred' or 'uncentred'. People who are centred feel tranquil, calm, serene, balanced and have peace of mind. In other words they are not indulging in any of the defence mechanisms we talked about earlier, in order to hide inner conflicts and inadequacies. People whose lives are centred show the following characteristics:

- reliability
- honesty
- integrity
- the courage to make commitments
- no need to be right about everything, all the time
- ability to give 100 per cent
- they're comfortable to be around
- self-respect

- calm dignity
- feel alive and powerful
- unlimited thinking.

These people have achieved a balance, a centre, between the drives pushing them in different directions, and have recognised and accepted the instincts and expectations that motivate their behaviour. They have achieved a life-style – job, social and family life – which satisfies, rather than clashes with, their fundamental needs. In a business situation, the centred person can bring creativity, problem solving, sensitivity and dedication to a situation, without complicating the issues with personal insecurities and anxieties.

In contrast, off-centre or uncentred individuals, have not accepted or recognised the different parts of their own personalities, or feel that they have not fulfilled their own potential – they've let themselves down, or cheated themselves in some way. They are:

- upset or angry
- anxious or frightened
- tense rather than calm
- off-balance instead of balanced
- unreliable
- dishonest
- of low integrity
- without the courage to make a commitment
- terrified of being wrong
- always holding back, unable to give 100 per cent
- very uncomfortable to be around.

33

Centred people have the opportunity to achieve excellence, uncentred individuals can only achieve mediocrity. Both states can change, or be changed. The centred individual can become complacent, can slip from the current state of contentment, can find that the real world ceases to meet expectations – someone who has fulfilled a job role happily and competently for a time can be jolted into misery and non-productivity by a new regime, a new boss or fears of insecurity. A good manager may be able to help the uncentred individual to confront and deal with at least some of the conflicts within himself, or between himself and the real world, which cause him to become off-balance. Centring (discussed further in Chapter 10) can only be achieved by recognising and acknowledging the truth.

Needs and motivation

Any pet-owner will tell you that his or her furry companion has a distinct personality and set of characteristic behaviours. But, if pressed, most will agree that these centre around the animal's attempts to fulfil a few basic needs – food, sleep, warmth, shelter, safety, elimination of wastes, and sex. It's the rare hungry cat or dog that will leave its food bowl for a pat from its owner! This is the most basic level of need, and although not many people in Western society have to concentrate solely on fulfilling such needs, it is still important to remember that a threat at this level is a threat to the most basic requirements of life. Telling a manager with a large mortgage and several children that she is to head up a potentially risky venture which could be shut down within a few months, is likely to meet with more enthusiasm if you state very directly that the manager's job and salary is *not* on the line if the initiative fails!

The things we 'need' can be arranged into a pyramid (see Figure 2.1), with basic bodily needs at the bottom, moving up to the requirement for safety, through the requirements for love, esteem and, at the top, the need for self-fulfilment. We have to have the bottom layers of the pyramid in place before we can move up and try to achieve the higher levels. Achievement of any of these needs can be fragile, and many people never attain the top of the pyramid, or reach it only for brief periods in their lives. You could consider that the process of moving up the pyramid is a process of personal growth, and that we have different pathways up it, and different goals at the top.

> **Taking risks with our abilities is the key to creation; playing it safe leads to stagnation.**

For some people, achieving the love and esteem of a few close individuals is the main goal of their lives, and maintaining that love provides all the self-fulfilment they require. This is typical of Nurses in the Human Technology system, and has a major impact on their relationships in the workplace. Once they've given their loyalty and affection to certain managers, colleagues or staff, they'll support and nurture those individuals to the utmost of their powers. But at the same time they find it difficult to criticise those people, or even to look at their work objectively. Nurses will never willingly upset one of their 'love-objects', because they will not want to risk losing their love in return. Unthinking loyalty can be as dangerous for a leader in business as opposition by subordinates. At the same time, Nurses find it hard to take day-to-day criticisms from those in whom they've placed their affection, and their response to any such 'attacks' will be hurt ('How could he say that to me? I thought he *liked* me!'), plus retaliation.

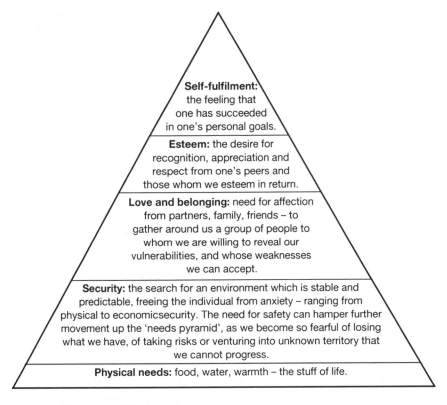

Self-fulfilment: the feeling that one has succeeded in one's personal goals.

Esteem: the desire for recognition, appreciation and respect from one's peers and those whom we esteem in return.

Love and belonging: need for affection from partners, family, friends – to gather around us a group of people to whom we are willing to reveal our vulnerabilities, and whose weaknesses we can accept.

Security: the search for an environment which is stable and predictable, freeing the individual from anxiety – ranging from physical to economicsecurity. The need for safety can hamper further movement up the 'needs pyramid', as we become so fearful of losing what we have, of taking risks or venturing into unknown territory that we cannot progress.

Physical needs: food, water, warmth – the stuff of life.

Fig. 2.1 The pyramid of needs

NEEDS IN DIFFERENT CULTURES

Different cultures place different emphases on different levels in the pyramid. In the USA, for example, the focus is on the individual and his or her personal growth and achievement, while Japan, for instance, emphasises the role of the group. In Japan, the success of the peer group is the ultimate goal, and each individual within the group shares the satisfaction of the group achievement. Individuality, which shows itself in forms of behaviour contradictory to group norms, and as potentially damaging to the group, is frowned upon. This makes the job of placing group (or company, in our case) goals at the top of people's list of aspirations, much easier in Japan than in the USA. The tradition of admiration for the maverick, the single achiever, the one 'out on a limb', is very strong in the USA. The right to assert one's individuality is deeply engrained, and attempts to restrict or direct such expressions is felt as a blow to one's self-esteem.

We'll discuss conflicts between group and personal goals later on, but it's worth pointing out here that this sort of cultural difference is one reason why attempts to implement good ideas from other countries can sometimes fall flat on their faces. Some Western companies have tried to introduce the sort of 'quality circles' common in Japan, for example, and found it difficult to understand their sluggish performance or outright failure.

Quality circles are small (typically 12-member) groups of people all working in the same part of a company, who meet regularly to discuss working practices, quality controls, how to improve productivity or the product itself. They are common in both manufacturing and in service industries. They are not just a forum for complaint and debate – they work on the basis that within the quality circle all individuals have equal input, and an equal responsibility for creative input. It is interesting that in a Japanese company a product rarely emerges at the end of a production process looking the same as it did when the planners and designers passed over their final blueprints. The product, and the process for producing it, is constantly changed in response to suggestions from the quality circles. Even once a production process has been set up and the end-products are going out to customers, the re-evaluation continues and the product and processes may continue to evolve.

A fully-functioning quality circle depends on all its members putting aside personal goals and adopting the goals of the circle and the company as a whole. So blame for errors or poor performance is accepted equally by all members of the circle, and everyone concentrates on removing the cause of the problem. Conversely, a good idea for better performance is presented to the circle to refine and improve, and then forwarded to senior management – all members of the circle take the credit equally.

Action

Remember: self-knowledge is the greatest form of knowledge. Rethink your own position with respect to the needs pyramid. Question: how much of what you do is motivated by your own needs factors? Is your search to fulfil your personal needs in conflict with corporate needs? Can you allow others space for personal growth without threatening your own?

Action

Training: encourage colleagues to consider each other's personal circumstances, needs and goals – but not to intrude into people's personal lives.

Action

Training: insecurity can be completely debilitating, preventing the person concerned from making any move they perceive as a potential risk. Help colleagues to identify and communicate sources of insecurity, which may be ill-founded and removable, once known.

Real-life experience

Adult, fully-functioning people are a complex mixture of inheritance, instinct, the conscious and subconscious, shaped and formed by the sum of all the experiences of their lives. Parents, teachers, peers and role-models all played their parts in building up the person you are, or work with. We started this chapter with the idea that the greatest knowledge you can find is self-knowledge and, for an adult, the self is really the sum of everything you've experienced. When assessing your (or others') reactions, abilities, choices and preferences, a most useful method is to remember, re-examine and analyse the past:

- What happened?
- Who was involved?
- What did I feel about what was happening?
- What would have made my behaviour different?
- With hindsight, did I behave in a logical fashion, or did I react emotionally – did I act for the best?

37

To some extent, we do this all the time. 'Normal' personality development relies on the process of analysing one's behaviour, and changing one's view of the world in the light of what we've learned, continuing all through life.

In the Human Technology system, it's the Generals who implement this best – and it's one of the reasons why they make good leaders. They are able to separate out facts and emotions. Nurses, on the other hand, find it hard to disentangle facts, actions and words from the way they, as the recipients, felt about them. They are often swamped by the emotion and pain of experiences. Also, if you ask a Nurse about an emotionally charged incident – say a meeting where either the Nurse, or one of her close circle, came in for criticism – you will find that the Nurse remembers the incident very differently from others present at the same meeting. For the Nurse, this 'distorted' experience will become what she remembers, and the scenario that is referred back to when dealing with the same people, or similar or related situations. This can be most confusing, and damaging, to others who have a different memory of the incident, and can lead to progressive divisions, misunderstandings and conflict.

Self-imposed limits

Each of us works up a series of 'rules' about the world, our own place in it, other people's behaviour, and our reactions to it. These rules are based on our own experiences and our analyses of these and are called 'personal constructs'. This is a useful idea, and many personality assessment tests have been compiled that make use of it. You can make use of it yourself, however, both to get to know your own library of personal constructs, and to get some idea of those of others.

The system works like this:

1 Think of three people – either real people or 'stereotypes', like 'someone *I admire*'; 'someone *I find threatening*'; 'someone *I feel sorry for*'.
2 Now think of opposing pairs of characteristics that you can use to compare and contrast them. These are the constructs. For example:
   ■ Sara and Helen are friendly to me, Jim is unfriendly
   ■ Sara and Jim are outgoing, Helen is shy
   ■ Jim and Helen are clever, Sara is not.
3 Carry on doing this both with other real people and with stereotypes.
4 Add yourself into the list of people.
5 Then sit back and consider both the kinds of constructs you've come up with, and how the constructs you've applied to people group together.
6 Have you aligned yourself with people you admire and like? Have you grouped certain characteristics as 'weak'; 'strong'; 'good'; 'bad'; 'successful'; 'failures'?
7 Now try and apply this to the people you are working with – first of all, do you know enough about them to do such an exercise? Do this quickly – you might be surprised by what you find you know and feel about colleagues!

We'll return to an approach like this in Chapter 4, when we discuss how to apply Human Technology to ourselves and the people we work with.

People's personal constructs make up a framework of how they see the world, and where they fit into it. Challenges to this framework may result in:

■ guilt
■ anxiety
■ threat and/or
■ hostility.

Guilt

Knowledge that the 'self' you are now, is no longer the 'self' you thought you were. For instance, if part of your framework is that you are an

UNDERSTANDING WHAT MAKES PEOPLE TICK

easy-going, well-liked social person, and your job role means that you have to take responsibility for disciplining staff who don't perform properly, you'll feel guilt over the mismatch.

Anxiety

Awareness that important events fall outside one's own framework, making it almost impossible to predict and plan for the future – such as when you're asked to do a job you feel you don't have the knowledge for.

Threat

Realisation that your framework is no longer adequate for the reality around you – for example when your professional life has been based around a particular set of skills, now no longer needed because of changes in technology.

Hostility

Refusing to accept that a prediction or expected event has failed to emerge, and continuing to try and change events to fit the original framework – such as hiring someone to do a particular job, and instead of accepting that their skills are simply not right, continuing to push them into your original conception.

Conflict arises when people's views of the world are upset in this way, but this is not always a bad thing. Personal construct systems can become rigid and unyielding, not moving with changes in the times and circumstances. Sometimes they are based on false assumptions, or assumptions which are out of date: 'I can't take on the running of that committee – I don't have the detailed knowledge needed and anyway I've got too much on my plate with the day-to-day work of the department!', may have been true in the first year of the person's employment, but is less likely five years later with several juniors to delegate to!

Chalkcheese Ltd – in walks Patrick

Following their first, rather inconclusive meeting, the members of the think-tank have all been mulling over what was said. A second meeting is scheduled for a week after the first, starting at 9.30am. By 9.15 Stuart, Natalie and Gail are gathered in the meeting room.

Natalie: I thought I'd bring along some coffee and biscuits for this meeting – shall we have some now, while we're waiting for Patrick?

Gail: That's a good idea. We can get comfortable before we start. Perhaps you'd both like to be reading through the notes I took last week? I've also prepared a suggested 'plan of campaign' to canvas the departments for their ideas about the computer solutions – you might like to think about it.

At 9.40 they are still waiting for Patrick.

Stuart: This is just what I expected – we're all thinking about Patrick's ideas, and Gail's done a lot of work trying to turn his giddy notions into practical strategies, and he can't even be bothered to turn up!

Gail: Well, let's begin. Now, what I'd like to do at this meeting is to prepare a questionnaire that we can give to all the heads of departments, asking them for any thoughts about how they'd like to amend their work practices to improve communications, save time, increase quality, and save money. They should fill these in together with key members of their teams. We'll use those to select the right system.

Stuart: How will we know what's available?

Gail: Well, I've got a list of computer consultants in this area. I'm checking them out now – taking up references and getting recommendations from other companies who've used them . . .

At this point the door opens and in walks Patrick.

Patrick: Oh, good, you're all here. I've got someone coming in at 10.30 – Cliff Thompson, from 'Tecsol'. He's a computer consultant I play golf with – just the man to tell us what we need . . .

After the first think-tank meeting, Stuart was fed up with trying to act as chairperson. He felt at sea, and had no idea how to proceed. He was relieved to see that Gail had come prepared with a plan, and happy to follow her lead.

Gail has been trying to catch hold of Patrick's suggestions and pull them together into some sort of ordered framework. She wants to proceed step-by-step, making sure all the ground is covered. She feels she's the only person in the think-tank likely to do this, so came into the second meeting much more determined to take control and set the agenda than she did in the first meeting.

But Patrick has now pre-empted all her careful planning! He paid no attention to her attempts to formalise and implement his suggestions, and has gone ahead on his own.

Experiences lead to behaviour, which leads to experiences

People respond to situations, to their environment, and to others, but at the same time they create and contribute to those situations. Then the experiences they undergo feed back into their personalities, modifying their behaviour (see Figure 2.2). People make judgements of their abilities, and having attempted tasks in line with those judgements, may revise them. They assess their performance on their own internal scales, as well as on the reactions of others, and will grade their successes and failures on many different levels.

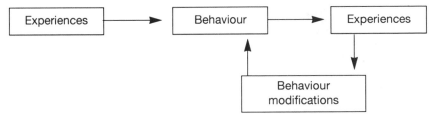

Fig. 2.2 The experience/behaviour loop

People work like problem-solving mechanisms, trying to behave in ways which maximise both their rewards from the outside world and the internal pat on the back when the individual feels they've done their best and achieved their goal.

Sometimes the sum of people's experiences and inner conflicts leads them to take a rather pessimistic approach to life – expecting the worst, always predicting that new plans will cost more, take longer, and require more people and resources than have been allocated. When this adds to a thorough, practical, cautious approach it can be invaluable in someone whose work role is one of attention to detail and fine tuning.

DEFENSIVE PESSIMISM AND SELF-FULFILLING PROPHECIES

Defensive pessimism is dangerous – this is the situation in which people are so afraid of failure that they predict a project will fail, so that at least they can be right in their prediction! A business can't afford to listen to these self-fulfilling prophecies – if a scheme will fail if not enough planning time is allocated to it, and then fails for that very reason, you'll have no idea if it might have succeeded if given adequate resources. And you've had no chance to test the ideas and organisational skills of the others involved in the project.

In cases of defensive pessimism it is important to recognise and deal with real concerns and potential problems, and to isolate the insecurities and anxieties of the pessimist. Then it's important to try and help her to recognise these and talk about them. Simply expressing her worries may be enough to make the pessimist realise that these are not as important as she feared. On the other hand, once you know what the concerns are, you may be able to give her assurances that what she fears will not happen, or that she will be helped. Or you may be able to give her more information if she feels in the dark.

Performers are never pessimists about their own ideas – and more likely than not will be carried along with those originating with others, as long as they see their chance to make at least some part of it their own challenge. If anything, they tend in the other direction – to eternal optimism!

Rewards and punishments

Why do we work? Well, it's obvious – to earn a living, or a better living. But that's not the only reason, or why do some of us choose to undertake very demanding jobs, work more hours than we're paid for, do voluntary unpaid work and retire with reluctance? Because there's more to work in the Western world than simply a good day's pay for a good day's labour.

42

For one thing, few of us are paid a day's pay for a day's labour – we're paid a monthly salary, which is not immediately related to how hard or effectively we've strived for it. If you have a bad month, distracted by personal problems or illness, your salary doesn't drop. In the long term you might be risking losing your job, or at least missing out on the next pay rise or promotion. But how then can we keep up the enthusiasm, creativity, energy and sense of responsibility needed to do our jobs at peak performance? If you reward a child or an animal for doing something that you want them to do regularly, you provide the reward immediately they've done what you want, and not at all if they don't come up to scratch. So, should we reward only good work, and pay less for inadequate performance?

In fact, the salary we get from working is only one of a whole series of 'rewards'. It's important – without it, we can't fulfil the needs at the base of our needs pyramid (food, shelter, security and so on). And it provides one means of defining and measuring status. But there are many more immediate rewards from day to day, which appeal to our higher needs, such as self-fulfilment, achievement of friendship and affection, increased respect and approval, the feeling of being part of a group.

Punishment is the reverse of reward – the stick as opposed to the carrot. Again thinking of children and animals, punishment is a very effective discouragement of unacceptable behaviour. There are problems with its effective use, for example, whereas rewarding desirable behaviour should (if properly and promptly done) encourage the recipient to repeat or continue the behaviour, punishment just tells the recipient that he or she has done wrong, not how to do right. Misapplied punishment is more likely to cause than to cure conflict – people resent punishment they see as unfair if they don't understand the reasons for it, or feel they've been singled out for blame when one or more others contributed to the behaviour or event that's being punished.

In the Human Technology system, the different weightings rewards and punishments have for the different characters give valuable clues as to how to get the best from them, and how to ensure smooth progress. 'Intangible' rewards might include:

Generals:	Problems successfully solved, clear plans laid down, installation of smooth-running systems.
Nurses:	Success of individual they support, gratitude for and recognition of support, sense of contentment and happy atmosphere.
Performers:	Public acclaim, new challenges, opportunity to 'win' in competition, being the star on the team.
Soldiers:	Targets achieved, sense of job completed, no loose ends.

43

All of these 'intangible' rewards rely on someone conveying messages of approval – communicating success. As we've seen from what's gone before in this chapter, we are all at the mercy of conflicting internal messages, and even the most confident of souls suffers some insecurity and anxieties. Communication is the most important tool in the Human Technology system, and the first defence against conflict. As well as communicating clear goals, it's also vital to communicate rewards – even hard-headed analytical Generals or effervescent Performers need out-side feedback on how well they are doing and whether their efforts are appreciated.

UNDERSTANDING WHAT MAKES PEOPLE TICK – A CHECKLIST

- The greatest knowledge is self-knowledge.

- Human Technology groups people into four types, based on their dominant personality traits: Generals, Nurses, Performers and Soldiers.

- Behaviour is a combination of instinct, learned rules, and experiences. Internal conflict between these can lead to external conflict.

- Human needs and drives can be organised into a pyramid – you have to achieve the bottom layers (food, shelter, security) before you can try and achieve the higher levels (peer accolades, self-fulfilment).

- Reassessing past experiences and your behaviour can mean you behave more successfully in the future, and help you to recognise behaviour traits in others, and predict what they are likely to do.

- Rewards are better strategy than punishments if your aim is to change people's behaviour or get the most appropriate behaviour from them.

- Communication is the most important Human Technology tool, and the first line of defence against conflict.

Human Technology: Generals, Nurses, Performers and Soldiers

The Chalkcheese team and Human Technology

Human Technology practitioners would have plenty of material to work with at the think-tank meetings! All four members of the team have something to contribute to the discussion, which is why they were selected. But they are all rubbing each other up the wrong way, each expecting the other three to behave in the same way as they would themselves.

Patrick is predominantly a **Performer**. He is creative, volatile, impatient of time constraints, rules, and hierarchies.

Gail, predominantly a **General**, is organised, logical and likes structure and a planned approach. She's thrown by Patrick's sudden changes of direction.

Stuart, the **Soldier**, is not really happy taking charge, especially when the project is open-ended and fuzzy. He's hard working and thorough, likes order and clear guidelines.

Natalie is predominantly a **Nurse**. She is a warm, supportive person, easily upset by conflict and confrontation. She is also creative and instinctive, but cowed by direct challenges and wary of revealing her vulnerabilities.

I first introduced the Human Technology system in Chapter 2, and in this chapter I want to explain the four main types in more depth. The elements of individual behaviour that we looked at in Chapter 2 (instinct, social rules, value systems and experiences) all add up together to form our individual characteristics – the things that make each of us special, and distinct from all others. But behavioural traits can be grouped together, giving a broad sketch of an individual's personality. Looking at a person's behavioural traits and grouping them together to form a complete picture, helps us to understand and predict their behaviour.

If you have an idea of how someone is likely to react to a new idea, a difficult situation, criticism or punishment, that will help you to develop a strategy for proceeding that is the least likely to set up barriers, or to be ineffective. This is a vital tool in avoiding the development of friction and conflict. At the same time, when trying to resolve a conflict situation, analysing the types of people involved can give crucial insights into the real causes of what is happening.

As discussed in Chapter 2, the four types are named 'Generals', 'Nurses', 'Performers' and 'Soldiers'. Performers are generally male, and Nurses female, whereas both sexes are fairly equally represented among Soldiers and Generals. It should also be reiterated that the category names may have little to do with an individual's real-life job title. A summary of the major characteristics of the four types, together with some suggestions for ideal jobs for each of them, is set out in Table 3.1.

As well as this dominant signature of the personality of each of us, we are, in addition, 'controlled' to a lesser degree by another of the four types – the minor or secondary component of our personality. There are people who are almost exclusively dominated by one character type. More often, however, the balance between major and minor components is less clear-cut and we need to ascribe careful weightings to each. This becomes especially relevant as the balance between components begins to change during the middle years of our lives – a topic discussed towards the end of this chapter. However, before embarking on some of these detailed applications of Human Technology, let's start by examining the central characteristics of Generals, Performers, Soldiers, and Nurses.

Generals

The thinkers, the organisers, the practical people of this world: these are our 'Generals'. Observations suggest that this personality type is shared equally between men and women, and both masculine and feminine stereotypes contain characteristics of the General type. The campaigning real-life general and the efficient mother organising the school run are drawing equally on the General's resources of logic, reason and rationality, together with skills of forward planning, attention to detail, communication and delegation.

CORE CHARACTERISTICS OF GENERALS

These are:

- organised, orderly

Table 3.1

Character	Key characteristics	Ideal business role
General	Organiser, a team leader, goal-oriented, structured, logical, numerate, responsible	Goal provider, policy-maker, financial controller, accountant, lawyer, running a business
Nurse	Supportive, disorganised, intuitive, creative, prickly, considerate, vulnerable	Real-life nurse, teacher, carer, secretary, support role
Performer	Visionary, intuitive, charismatic, egotistical, creative, independent, illogical, spontaneous, unstructured	Producer of new ideas, new business provider, client cultivator, salesperson, marketeer, public relations
Soldier	Team player, solid, unimaginative, uncomplicated, consistent, patient	Goal executor (turning policy into reality), manager, long-term employee

47

- desire for power
- goal-oriented
- stubborn, to the point of being rigid, brittle
- factual
- do not like change – agents for consistency
- literate, numerate
- good communicators
- comfortable making decisions and telling others what to do
- manipulative
- like rules and regulations

- professional
- detailed and meticulous
- reliable
- authoritative, autocratic, imperious
- do 'the right thing'
- educated and academically oriented
- do not suffer fools at all – let alone gladly
- blinkered
- linear thinkers
- team leaders
- individualistic
- do not like risk
- structured, hardworking.

Generals don't believe in luck: their motto might be 'you reap what you sow'. They value material possessions, public recognition of merit, and are happiest working in well-defined structures or hierarchies. Generals love debate. It may be that they feel so secure in their own opinions that they run little risk of being swayed by the arguments of others, or that they do not feel personally challenged or emotionally attacked by someone disagreeing with them. Writing (apart from poetry), teaching, accounting and the law are typical General professions, and there is no doubt that Generals make good leaders.

They think things through, set clear goals and establish paths to reach them. Rules and regulations are laid down and adhered to, which provide these people with a sort of naturally protected personal space, within which they may be very private people. It's not that they don't mix well with others – they are in fact good at articulating their message, well able to outline their thoughts, opinions and plans clearly and convey them to workmates, employees, friends and family. But Generals do have trouble appreciating that others may not be as single-minded or meticulous as themselves, or may be motivated by rewards other than the purely material.

Once set on a course, it is not always easy to persuade Generals to change direction. If external conditions alter, they will not be the first to perceive how this should affect their behaviour. Indeed, even rational arguments supported by factual evidence – two commodities highly valued by this group – may not be enough to convince them of the need for change. A fondness for repetitious tasks and old habits can be a difficulty for Generals who use their intellect to guide them through life. They think their way out of problems, whereas Performers act their way out, Soldiers fight their way out and Nurses cry their way out. It is easy to think of Generals as stubborn and blinkered, but these are only other aspects of characteristics which also reveal themselves in perseverance and organisation. Nevertheless, stubbornness is often taken to the point of becoming rigid, and then Generals' thinking can become a weakness rather than a strength.

In a work situation they will be discomforted by attempts to set up 'brainstorming' sessions, or to introduce more 'organic' methods of management. However, all Generals shine in meetings – they are happy to take the floor and expound or defend an idea. Taking the chair, they will insist on the agenda being followed rigidly, refusing to allow skipping from point to point. Instructions to subordinates will always be clear and comprehensive, but at the same time may be inflexible and tactless. Generals can lack people skills – they will not always be the best at coaxing out the hidden talents of a shy or difficult colleague. It's easy for them to overlook or underrate the abilities of others, and they place a low value on suggestions founded on intuition or emotion.

Generals are common at managerial level in business. It's also helpful to think of there being various categories – I call them one-, two-, three-, or four-star Generals. There are lots and lots of one-star generals around – they don't really aspire to any great deeds. They acknowledge that there is a higher authority than themselves, and their ambitions are modest, and they are happy with the situation – indeed, they represent the bulk of the population and do not cause conflict. The arena for conflict occurs between the four-star and the three-star Generals – between different styles of leadership.

49

The effective management style of Generals can be broken down into four components. They:

- receive and provide information
- educate
- direct
- delegate.

A simple example of the four stages of authority, might be how I, as a General, would arrange to set up my preferred refreshment procedure when being visited by clients.

Say my secretary brought in coffee for a meeting between myself and a client – plus a plate of custard creams and digestives. Now, I like custard creams but I don't like digestives, but to my horror there was only one custard cream and the client ate it. If I was a General, I would say to my secretary:

'Look, this is how I would like it done in the future: I want two plates of biscuits. One should have four custard creams on it and that plate is for me; the other should have a selection of biscuits and that is to be placed in front of my client. That way, we will both end up with what we want.'

Now, once I have given her this information, and told her why I want things done this way, it makes me feel good, and it provides a better service to my clients. This is **provision of information** and **education**, and the third stage is **direction**. So the next time I have a meeting, I say to my secretary, 'You remember the coffee-time procedure we talked about?' She says, 'Yes.' I know she knows exactly how I want it to be, and I can **delegate** that job to her.

This is what Generals do – there is a process they have to go through that relates to both the trivial and the important things in life. The General who achieves this feels great – empowered and in control. My secretary will also feel great because, rather than sensing I wasn't happy with something, but not knowing what, she is absolutely clear about what's wanted and is able to get it precisely right. Generals with these authoritative qualities need to exercise them, practise using them, and not be frightened of saying how they want things to happen – Generals have a responsibility to train their troops. The key is the ability to communicate.

> **What you are unwilling to communicate runs you.**

Performers

Performers are the actors and entertainers in the Human Technology system. They are the most flexible of the four types, the most chameleon-like, and can play any role. The other three types are more fixed, and more consistent and predictable. Performers are magicians, who constantly pull rabbits out of hats, surprising and exasperating everyone around them.

CORE CHARACTERISTICS OF PERFORMERS

These are:

- charismatic
- inspiring
- motivating, exciting
- love control, but hate the responsibility that goes with it
- they want status, unlike Generals who want power

- do best when their backs are to the wall
- 'fire-fighting' life style
- have little self-discipline
- need guidance
- not team players
- shoot from the hip, often frightening to others
- entrepreneurs
- need change, action, movement
- risk takers
- sociable
- emotional
- unprofessional
- always centre stage, holding court
- life is a drama
- hopeless time and money keepers
- see tasks in terms of missions
- poor discernment skills
- hate rules, regulations and discussion
- poor planners
- poor communicators
- agents of change
- unstructured
- artistic
- imaginative
- don't perceive risk
- irrational, blameless
- great storytellers (often lie a lot!).

51

The main point to be highlighted in relation to these traits is that Performers' behaviour is to a large extent spontaneous and intuitive – their actions, decisions and opinions tend to spring from an emotion-based 'gut feeling' about any particular situation. They are not reflective, organised or logical in the way they respond to events.

Performers (the majority of whom are men) are inspirational, flamboyant, larger-than-life characters who thrive on change and react spontaneously to it. They live life at a much faster pace than others – a fact illustrated by reading the biography of almost any successful entrepreneur. Typically, they made their first million when they were 21 years old, lost it when they were 22, regained it and got married at 23, were divorced and started a new business at 24, and so it goes on.

Performers are very good at coming up with new ideas but are not very good at selecting which of the ideas are worth pursuing. They have no aptitude for formalised project appraisal, drawing up cash-flow forecasts, competitor analysis and so forth – for them commercial decisions are based on instinct, not careful evaluation, logic and planning. Engaging Performers in detailed discussions about their plans, or indeed anything else, is likely to be a waste of time – they prefer to 'hold court' and to impress their view on to others. Emotional and passionate, they act rather than think their way through life.

Time-keeping ability – or rather the lack of it – is another important characteristic that marks out Performers. If you give a General a nine-to-five job, then, as with any other form of orderly structure, he or she will feel secure within it. Performers feel trapped by a structured existence – they work odd hours, and living and working with them can be very demanding. Their volatility keeps all around them constantly on their toes. Exciting, yes, but also unnerving, exhausting and often time-wasting. The Performer is so full of ideas, leaping from one to another with barely a break in between, that the more pedestrian may be left behind in confusion.

Sometimes lacking balance and judgement, but seldom personal charm and a highly persuasive manner, they may plunge into a catastrophic course without due consideration, taking others with them. Change for its own sake may be visited on long-suffering colleagues and family, who have little opportunity for discussion with the Will-o'-the-wisp who won't stand still long enough to receive input from others or debate possible alternative courses.

Performers start many things but rarely finish any of them. When they get bored, they find it hard to carry on with routine but necessary tasks. Everything has to be fresh – always new – a challenge. Sometimes the economics of this can be disastrous, resulting in a huge investment of resources in new developments – unprofitable change for the sake of change. In many ways the Performer works best as a one-man-band. He hates to sit in meetings, is too impatient to explain his ideas clearly to others and can't be tied down to a routine. In short, he is not a team player and the best course is usually to acknowledge this, give him his own department and a title, and he will perform miracles.

Performers make particularly good sales people and new business developers and they flourish best if a special structure is created in which they can operate independently as a potential source of profit. An important point is *not* to give them any people for whom they are responsible or any problems to solve – Performers are useless at running a team, or anything else, and rather than solving problems they tend to create them.

Due to their outgoing nature, few people realise how insecure and vulnerable Performers really are. This leads to their great highs and depression-induced lows, which sometimes create a susceptibility to drugs and alcohol.

A coat of paint in the car park

One of my clients in Los Angeles was a $40 million turnover hospital complex, the Norfolk Medical Centre. In the US, of course, medical centres are commercial enterprises and are supposed to make a profit. Norfolk was just breaking even. So a new chief executive, Robert, was brought in, and given the task of improving profits.

Robert's primary component was that of a Performer, an entrepreneur, not fundamentally interested in the internal workings of the Centre, but who concentrated on how to present the facility most successfully to the community, and attract patients and funding. Robert's assistant director, a woman called Agnes, was predominantly a General. Robert complained interminably about being totally misunderstood by his board of directors.

53

I went to see him one day and he came charging in, furious. He said, 'I've been complaining for weeks that the lines marking parking spaces in the car park are all faded and disgusting, so I yelled at the maintenance people and got three of them to repaint the whole area immediately. This kind of sloppiness is very bad for the image of the hospital – it's the first thing people see when they come in.' He was very proud about it.

Agnes, his assistant director, who really ran the place, was appalled, and said so. Robert couldn't understand why. She said, 'Three months ago you signed an order to have the whole hospital repainted, which we do every two years. The painters are starting on Monday, and the car park lines are part of the contract. The three people you've got painting lines were cleaning medical equipment ahead of a heavy schedule of operations at the weekend.'

He said, 'Oh! No one told me the painters were coming in on Monday!' Agnes replied in frustration, 'But *you* signed the order and anyway, it's your job to run the hospital – you should not have to be reminded of this major, very expensive event – the complete redecoration of the hospital!' So she went out, feeling very, very upset, leaving Robert equally upset. He said, 'They just do not understand me.' That's when I said, 'Well you're a Performer', and ran through the Human Technology model with him.

We build a framework of assumptions and expectations about others. The assistant director, who was a General, was very organised, full of details, planned, responsible. She applied those expectations on to her director saying, 'That's what you should be. We are running a huge business here and you should be organised, systematic and careful.' He was none of those things. He was irresponsible, unreliable and no good at details. Any information you gave him went in one ear and out the other, but she still continued to expect those qualities from him. His constant failure to fulfil her expectations caused her to become very stressed at work. At the same time Robert was exasperated because he knew what Agnes expected of him, and some part of him agreed that those qualities are what could be expected of someone in his position, but he didn't want to admit it.

So the relationship was doomed. Rather than benefiting from each other's strengths, what they tended to do was to criticise each other's weaknesses: a destructive rather than a constructive and productive partnership.

Soldiers

Soldier-dominant personalities are reliable, hard working, supportive, dogged and loyal. Both sexes are equally represented in this category. He or she is practical and focused – the kind of person who is often referred to as 'good in a crisis', or 'a tower of strength'. They don't give way easily under stress, and will persevere, radiating calm and reassurance, while others are beginning to panic. It is not easy to sway a Soldier from his chosen path, although this very tenacity can be his downfall if he is short-sighted about the potential risks of persisting without change and adaptation to evolving conditions.

CORE CHARACTERISTICS OF SOLDIERS

These are:

- very supportive
- loyal, solid, stalwart
- persistent, reliable and rarely panic
- structured, stolid and plodding
- academia is a bit of a struggle
- thick-skinned
- bit of a bulldozer attitude through life – go through rather than around
- slow to grasp new concepts

- no ideas for themselves
- uninnovative
- need directing
- don't see need for change
- enjoy serving others and like to be led
- don't want limelight
- very hardworking
- factual
- good managers
- team players
- harmony is very important
- service is fulfilling.

Soldiers feel close to their environment, and need feedback from nature if they are to maintain their calm. These colleagues are the ones who come back rested and refreshed after a holiday watching birds from a damp hut on the marshes, or spending a weekend completely relandscaping their garden. They won't be the first to spot another's emotional dilemma, and may even contribute to it with tactless comments or out-of-place suggestions. But once a Soldier has given his loyalty and love to another individual, that person will have to do something remarkably hurtful to threaten that devotion.

Among the positive aspects of the Soldier's personality are reliability and consistency. Once given a clear direction, competent management and adequate training, the Soldier will apply policies, guidelines and principles thoroughly and comprehensively. These individuals care deeply about their work – and this applies to all projects they take on, whether in a commercial context, or hobbies, voluntary activities or jobs around the home. They are prepared to put in long hours, and will see the most complex or tedious tasks through to the bitter end, long after others have become bored, or despaired of ever completing them.

Soldiers can keep their attention on the job at hand – what's happening right now – rather than wasting time over pointless speculation about what might or might not happen in the future, or what might or might not have been in the past. An employer will gain the respect and loyalty of a Soldier by providing clear and competent leadership, while subordinates of Soldiers will be encouraged to form part of a smoothly functioning team. The Soldier gains satisfaction and reward from a job well done, not from scoring points off others, or shining as the brightest star in the group.

All the positive aspects of the Soldier's personality can be turned against him, however, if he fails, as he may easily do, to foresee obstacles in his path. The very tenacity and focus which enables him to follow a planned strategy without deviating tends to rule out the sort of far-sighted deductions characteristic of Generals, or the more intuitive leaps of Nurses and Performers. It's hard to turn a Soldier from his chosen path, even when it's clear to others that the path leads straight to disaster. Their impervious natures – which might unkindly be termed 'thick-skinned' – render them immune to criticism or ridicule. We have seen that, of the four groups, Performers go through life at the fastest pace: Soldiers are at the other end of the spectrum, operating at the slowest rate and are always society's 'late bloomers'.

While Performers and Generals represent two different styles of leadership, Soldiers and Nurses are two different styles of support. Performers provide a very charismatic, emotional, spontaneous, intuitive style of leadership, while the General is well-organised and authoritative. Similarly with support, Soldiers provide a factual, unemotional support style, while Nurses represent an emotional, nurturing style of support.

56

Nurses

Nurses are creative and artistic, in the same way as Performers, and are similarly capable of innovation, and intuitive leaps. They like to feel their lives are organic, flowing and changing in tune with the world around them. But, unlike Performers, they wither, rather than thrive, under pressure and stress.

CORE CHARACTERISTICS OF NURSES

These are:

- very unstructured
- very emotional
- very caring
- prickly
- hate confrontation with a passion
- creative, artistic
- intuitive
- supportive
- long suffering
- smothering, clinging

- feel victims of their circumstances
- feel wounded easily, defensive if under attack
- rarely feel in control – get 'lost' in life
- very affectionate, loving
- nurturing
- need to be part of 'a nest'
- have a lot to offer but need to be drawn out
- need to be directed, supported, loved.

Nurses, most of whom are women, don't see themselves as stars, and become self-conscious and insecure when put in the spotlight. In a crisis, a Nurse may lose her head, and become incapable of making decisions, requiring instead to be reassured and looked after by colleagues, family and friends. Nurses suffer greatly from the every-day knocks and spills of life. They take rejections and disappointments more to heart than others, and are unlikely to be able to stand up for their own beliefs or decisions in the face of opposition. At the same time, they are sensitised to the emotional pressures others may be under and can empathise with those caught on the horns of a business-versus-personal dilemma. They may also act as emotion amplifiers, spreading waves of their own emotional state among their workmates, passing on contentment or anxiety, dissatisfaction or well-being to all they come into contact with.

People with a large proportion of the Nurse in their personality make-up can provide a warm, cosy, loving centre to whatever organisation they may be in – family or business, large impersonal institution or tiny independent concern. They can bring to any group a sense of awareness of other's needs, making every individual feel special and cared for. As teachers and real-life nurses they are unsurpassed – even the dullest child will believe they are a worthwhile person, or the illest patient that they are on the road to recovery, if a Nurse tells them so.

These individuals thrive on compliments and affection, and will work both hard and effectively if they receive feedback from those around them, reassuring them that what they are doing is both right and appreciated. Their creative and artistic depths can sometimes supply novel solutions to problems or better approaches to long-established systems and traditions – as long as they feel secure enough to proffer their opinions without fear of rejection. Employers who can involve a Nurse in their planning and management teams will gain a valuable resource: antennae finely attuned to every emotional nuance among the staff and with deep-seated loyalty towards anyone who takes the time to gain their confidence and affection. Employees or subordinates of Nurses can have a wonderful time, cherished and protected, their skills

57

and ambitions recognised and nurtured, their emotional and personal problems treated sympathetically.

The other side of the coin is the stifling, cotton-wool atmosphere that a Nurse can gather around herself. A situation in which every word is carefully chosen to avoid hurting the feelings of others – and, most especially, of the Nurse herself. Children of a Nurse parent may never be able to escape the fussy, protective embrace, or the perpetual demands for reassurance and comfort. In a working situation, the Nurses can create havoc, magnifying and disseminating worry, anxiety, fear or discontent throughout previously smooth-running organisations. Employers and managers of Nurses must be constantly on their guard against unconscious slights and neglects. At the same time, they must remember the importance of coaxing the shrinking Nurse out of the shadows and into the vulnerable position of talking about her ideas and suggestions, daring possible criticism or ridicule.

Chalkcheese Ltd – the second think-tank meeting continues . . .

Cliff Thompson, the computer expert from Tecsol, has just left after a fairly disorganised discussion with the think-tank members. He obviously has no clear idea of what they expect from him, and they have been unable to brief him about what they want.

Gail: Patrick! How could you have invited Cliff to the meeting without consulting us first! We looked like complete fools, unable to give him any details about what we want!

Patrick: Look, I can't see what all the fuss is about! Surely you agree that we need a specialist? Of course we do – we're not up to the minute on what's available in the computer field, that's what Cliff's for. And I *have* briefed him. I told him all about Chalkcheese, and what we're doing. He's got enough to be working on.

Stuart: I completely disagree! You're a newcomer to the company, and your experience is all in marketing. You haven't got a fair overview of how the other departments work. I don't consider you competent to give a briefing to a consultant on your own. And where's your report of what you've said to him?

Patrick: Look, I'll write it up for you if you want – but I didn't give him a written briefing, just chatted about what's needed.

Stuart: You mean you've got nothing in writing?! And what did you arrange with him about fees?

Patrick: We didn't discuss that, I thought you could sort all that out. Another guy I play golf with told me Cliff's charges are very reasonable.

Gail: Oh my God! If you had your way, Patrick, we could all stay at home and this entire company would be run from the 'nineteenth hole' at your golf club! I don't often feel at a loss, but this all seems such a mess! How are we going to proceed from here?

Natalie: Couldn't we go ahead with your suggestion of questionnairing the heads of department about their development plans? Then we could give that information to Mr Thompson, and . . .

Stuart: That won't work! He's been given some half-baked idea by our resident whiz-kid, and won't pay any attention to us! No, as far as I'm concerned, Thompson has not been employed by this company and won't be.

Patrick: Don't call me a whiz-kid! I'm trying to get ahead with this project, to inject some new ideas and some enthusiasm into it. I don't know why I even bother!

Natalie: (who is almost in tears) I hate all this argument, and I don't seem to be able to make any useful contribution to this meeting – everything I suggest is useless! I want to resign! I'll ask my head of department to suggest someone else to represent customer services.

59

Major and minor components of behaviour

You're probably saying, 'This is too simple. You can't divide all of humanity into four types!' And no, it isn't quite that simple. Everyone has *two* of these four behavioural types within themselves – a primary and a secondary component.

The left brain represents logic, reason, fact, structure and is linear, while the right brain represents intuition, instinct, imagination, spontaneity, expansion and is creative. Generals and Soldiers are left brain; Performers and Nurses right brain (see Figure 3.1).

Most people have some contribution from both – people whose major component is 'General' and minor 'Nurse' are more common than people whose components are both right brain – say Performer-Nurses; or both left brain, Soldier-Generals. Our primary and secondary components may be present in any proportions. For example, I mentioned that Lady Thatcher is 90 per cent General, 10 per cent Nurse, making her a much tougher, more authoritarian character than John Major, who is 70 per cent General, 30 per cent Soldier.

Trying to engender a feeling of balance within ourselves as between our two component drives can be an unnerving process and a struggle. In addition, there's a change in emphasis from our secondary into our primary component as we mature. We'll discuss this later in the chapter (p.65).

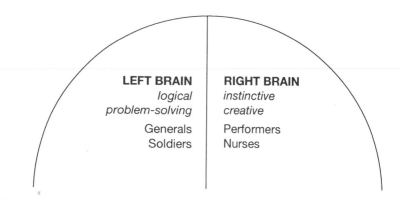

Fig. 3.1 Left-brain and right-brain traits

Both our primary and secondary components act (sometimes in concert, sometimes in opposition) to determine our behaviour in respect to new situations. Sometimes our secondary component will take us (and our colleagues!) by surprise, causing, for example, the competent, professional General to react with an out-of-character emotional outburst: for example, in the most recent Chalkcheese episode, Gail's reaction (Gail is a General-Nurse) having heard the views of yet another of Patrick's golfing chums. Habits, pressures and traditions in this country lead to the formation of an unusually high proportion of Generals, and a common player in the UK business world is the 'emotional General' – ie a General with the secondary component of Nurse.

MASCULINE vs FEMININE

As well as left-brain/right-brain divisions of traits there are also 'masculine/feminine' divisions of traits (see Figure 3.2). Masculine traits are *'outgoing'*, feminine traits are those that *'receive'*. Performers and Generals are 'masculine' in this sense: they are 'doers' and they tend to take charge of the world around themselves. Soldiers and Nurses are 'feminine': they receive from the world around them.

The most successful people in business life manage to both give and take. If you're giving all the time, not listening to ideas and

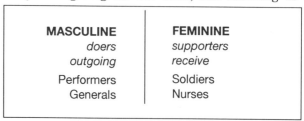

Fig. 3.2 Masculine and feminine traits

feedback from around you, you miss out on the best that others can provide. Creative fires need fuel and need to be fed with new ideas from all around. Your creative processes need substance with which they can join and merge, making something new and whole out of what the rest of the world sees as spare parts.

THE EMOTIONAL GENERAL

Just going through the characteristics of the four types in the

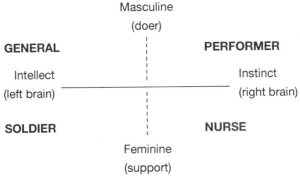

Fig. 3.3 A matrix of Human Technology traits

61

Human Technology system, you might be tempted to declare that 'All managers should be Generals'. But you'd be making a mistake. Sure, organisation, logic, planning, and decision making can be useful managerial traits. But an empathy with other members of staff, customers and suppliers can ease day-to-day business life, and be invaluable in situations of conflict. Someone who simply stands by his or her position in an argument with no concept of the pressures the opposition are under, or the emotional stress they may be feeling, can only contribute to, and escalate, the conflict.

Even more importantly, Generals (and Soldiers), who use their left brain predominantly, receive little input from their instincts. Indeed, they distrust and ignore 'gut feelings'. There is evidence to suggest that many of the best run companies in America today are those in which the management are trained to trust and then use their right-brain properties of intuition and instinct, rather than to manage by rote. In today's fast-changing world where we can't rely only on what we've learned and practised or what we can research in the time available, instinct may often be all we've got.

Performers and Nurses use and trust their instincts. They may not always be able to tell you *why* they act as they do – Performers won't see why you want to know, and Nurses will feel threatened by your questioning! But if you take a retrospective look at business situations in which someone's 'gut feeling' was followed, you'll be amazed at how often that turned out to be the right thing to do.

Cathy: Instead of combining both features in a single product, let's make two different products.

Bill: Why?

Cathy: Well, I don't really know, it just seems like a good idea . . .

Anita: It *is* a good idea – feature one is essential for the home market, but doesn't mean a thing in Europe, while feature two will go down really well in Germany and France, but most UK users haven't the capacity for it yet – we can really target our sales drive, without confusing the market with stuff about features they are not interested in.

Anita may have explained and detailed the idea – but would it have occurred to her in the first place? If the two separate products *are* a success – who should get the credit?

Many Generals have the secondary, right-brain component of a Nurse. One of the problems for male 'emotional Generals' in this country is the stress and pressure they suffer from not being able to express emotion. There is sociological and cultural pressure for 'keeping a stiff upper lip'. Stress, the pressure from unreleased emotion, can be temporarily released by various stress reduction techniques, but the emotion is still there, still being produced by the Nurse side of personality.

> **Stress is caused by keeping up a false image. Be yourself.**

I have come across many men in positions of authority, trying to practise being Generals, taking control, giving orders, making rules, ensuring that the regulations are met, but suffering a deficiency in their lives because they have never learned to acknowledge and feel comfortable with the emotional self that is the other half of their behavioural characteristic and of themselves.

THE PERFORMER-GENERAL (OR GENERAL-PERFORMER)

It is rather unusual to find people whose two components are different qualities of leadership. They may be Performer-Generals – ie, their primary component is Performer and their secondary General, or vice versa.

The Performer component represents an inspirational and erratic style of leadership – someone who suddenly has this idea that he *has* to do something. The Performer can be almost messianic. All of a sudden he thinks, '*That's* what I should do! I'm off !' In some ways, it's ludicrous – but very exciting, very charismatic. He can't keep it to himself, he can't stop to consult, consider – he spouts his piece, hoists his flag and off he marches! His audience, roused to fever pitch by the rhetoric and vision, are very excited by this, saying, 'This is wonderful, marvellous – a new tomorrow!', and they jostle to keep up with the prophet-Performer. Then you have the bulk of people thinking, 'That lot seem to know where they are going, let's follow them!' When they all get there, the Performer turns around and says, 'What are you lot doing here? I didn't say you should follow me' and he runs away and leaves them. This is OK at the truly entrepreneurial level, but can lead to huge trouble in more mature organisations.

The General style of leadership is quite different. First of all Generals stand still, which is a great advantage. They tend to act like orchestra conductors, looking at the group they're leading, making sure they all know the music, they're all wearing the same uniform, and that they are all in step. Generals pay attention to detail, and it works.

The downside of having two masculine components, is having no 'receive' component. So while someone who is in this category is very good at being an orchestra conductor or an entrepreneur, he is *not* very good at listening.

Most people are frightened of the Performer, because he is so charismatic and volatile. It's very difficult to get other people to talk to him. The Performer-General has an even more difficult position – the General in him desperately wants to work his way up through the organisation, while the Performer side breaks the rules and doesn't *want* to do the right thing.

THE GENERAL-SOLDIER

Prime Minister John Major is an example of the General-Soldier – someone who has no emotion component to his personality. He very rarely loses the plot: he is very steady, solid, and structured. You could say he was a bit of a 'Sherman tank' type, carrying on regardless, with great strength. What he does not see is that he may be going in the wrong direction. He needs someone with instinct – Performers or Nurses – to give him some vision and ideas. That is why he was very good for Lady Thatcher when he was part of her team. She was mostly General, but with some Nurse component – she had vision, and she utilised people like him. If I were advising John Major, I would say, 'You need a group of people you can consult, people you trust. They should be people, who are sympathetic to the vibrations and currents that are closed to you.'

Action

This is good advice for all Soldiers and Generals in positions of power – learn to use the instinctive, visionary skills of the Performers and Nurses on your team. Don't just squash them with your relentless logic – they have a 'feel' for things.

How the Soldier released the Performer inside him

At one company I worked with, there was a Performer-Soldier, a man called Thomas, who had been at the company for 20 years. The Soldier part of his personality had made him a loyal, supportive 'company man', but he'd had very little acknowledgment for his years of service.

64

Thomas was a tremendous salesman, but the business he was in was an old-established professional consultancy, and salesmen weren't appreciated or valued. He was particularly undervalued because he was rather outlandish and non-conformist – he never fitted in. His older brother had his own company, very high profile, and had always said to Thomas, 'Come and join me!'

For all sorts of reasons, Thomas has always said, 'No, I can't leave just now, it wouldn't be loyal, the company has done so much for me.' That was the Soldier in him speaking, saying, 'This is my army, I'm stuck here, committed, I can't move – it's against regulations.' But at the same time, the Performer part of him, which was growing stronger and stronger as time went on was telling him, 'I'm very frustrated! I'm not rewarded or appreciated, although I do all this business, bring in all these clients, all this income. So what if I'm a bit of a slob? OK, I don't wear the right tie or say the right thing, but that doesn't affect my contribution to this company, and still no one appreciates me.'

So when I went there I said 'Look, Thomas, this is what you must do. You have *got* to express your real skills – make them known. You're a Performer, you're forty-four years old, you have got to let go. You've got to let the Soldier part of yourself – the loyal, head-down, order-following part of you – take a back seat, and give free rein to the creative, instinctive side of you.'

I spoke to the chairman of the company and said, 'Listen, you have to release Thomas from the restrictions of the rules and traditions of the company. If you want the best from him – and the best for the organisation – you have to let him become an independent player. Performers are not team men, so stop trying to fit him into all the different teams – he won't fit. Give him his own department, a special title, a good secretary, a nice office and a nice car, and let him get on with it. On his own, Thomas will produce masses of business for you. But, whatever you do, *don't* give him any people to be responsible for. He is no good at running anything.'

That's what they did, and Thomas now produces more business than all the rest of the company put together. He has got an impressive-sounding title, a fancy car and he's happy as a sandboy. He's blossoming! He was the classic square peg in a round hole, although for years he gave the appearance of someone willing to stay in that ill-fitting hole, however uncomfortably. His employers saw the sense of what I said, and gave him the square hole he needed. But if they hadn't sorted out the right kind of niche that allowed him to function fully, my advice to him would have been, 'Leave. This is not your army, and if you are not appreciated by the army don't stay in it.'

THE SOLDIER-NURSE

In all the years I've been using the Human Technology system, I've only ever met one person at a management level in business whose major and minor components were both the supportive components – he was predominantly a Soldier and his secondary component was Nurse. He was a surveyor, aged 51, in a large professional practice. He was an excellent surveyor, and very good at being supportive and nurturing, but was almost incapable of taking on any authority. Because of his age and experience, he'd been made leader of a section of five people. But really he was quite incapable of leading them, giving them orders or instructions – he couldn't reprimand them, and he wasn't able to educate them.

65

The only time that he proffered any information was if they came to him in desperation saying, *'Please*, tell me what I should do', or *'Please* help me, I've got a problem.' In response he might say, 'Well, you may want to consider this and this, etc', but he was really feeling, 'Don't ask me, don't listen to me, go and get help from someone else.' He didn't want to offer information or guidance, because he didn't feel he had the confidence and authority to advise others. As a result, he found life rather difficult.

In fact he was quite happy in a subservient role – he had no desire for any authority or to take on leadership. What he asked for was some more money, and this was granted in recognition of his solidarity, support and his loyalty. But even after this, he certainly wasn't paid as much as someone 20 years younger doing the same job, but taking more leadership responsibility.

Human Technology and the life cycle

I mentioned earlier that, as people reach mid-life, they experience a change in emphasis – a move away from the secondary component of their personality into their primary component. For many people this can be the cause of significant and potentially difficult problems and trauma in their lives. The trouble often stems from an unwillingness to admit what in reality we already know – that our primary component *is indeed* our primary component and that it's OK to feel more at ease with who we really are and to move into and to feel more comfortable with this primary aspect of our personality. Because of the importance of the transition and the difficulties it so often causes, I want to discuss it in detail in this section.

As we move through life, until about the age of 35, we mostly rely on our secondary component to 'sort life out' – to help us make decisions and solve problems. But around the 35 to 42 age range, we start to experience dissatisfaction with our 'lot' – what we are doing with our lives, the way we are tackling life, and the things we are getting out of it. Many people at this stage feel they want something different – feel that they want to re-evaluate who they are, what they are, what they do and how they do it.

Depending on our secondary component, this re-evaluation can happen relatively early or relatively late. For example, someone whose secondary component is a Soldier – who, as we have seen, has a much slower rhythm when progressing through life and who is a late bloomer – would not start thinking of changing, or moving from the secondary into their primary component (regardless of which that is) until much later than other types. In my experience, it can be up to seven years later than average before secondary-component Soldier-types are able to fully acknowledge, explore, and make use of their primary component.

For example, Prime Minister John Major is a General whose secondary component is that of a Soldier. He is still in the process of learning to shift his attitude from that of a Soldier – a supportive person who is good at taking orders and receiving direction – into that of a General, who gives orders, who can be authoritative, who can be dictatorial, and so on. In the same way, someone whose primary component is Performer (like Thomas in the case study on page 64), at the 'switch period' feels the need to break away from rules and regulations, to take centre stage, to create their own thing, and to seek out status and acknowledgement.

MATURITY AND MID-LIFE CRISES

In our early adult years, therefore, we learn maturity, self-sufficiency, self-authority, while in our early-thirties there is more focus on taking responsibility for others – families and work. Then comes a period of change of focus. The primary component demands fulfilment – Generals, for example, take stock of their achievements and compare them to those of their peers. 'I should be a director of this company by now', or, 'I should have started my own company.' Generals who feel they have secured what they've spent their adult lives working their way towards, get a great sense of achievement, which powers them onwards. Those who feel they haven't made it suffer from self-reproach and self-doubt.

If the two components in your personality are to be supportive and nurturing on the one hand, and to be authoritative and directing on the other, the only time that you will feel whole and complete, and therefore in control, is when you utilise *both* parts of yourself. It's only when people get in touch with their major component in life that they start to feel in control, mature, and balanced.

THE EMERGING GENERAL

Generals often sees glimpses of their later authoritarian drive, even in their formative years. This may take the form of dissatisfaction on the part of the General with the person in charge, and to whom she reports. She may feel that person is not very good at it and that she could do a better job. Also, not liking the morality of the leader is often a factor – feeling that the leader's style of leadership is autocratic and based on fear, dismissiveness, rudeness, nastiness, and feeling that if she were in charge she would not be like that.

THE EMOTIONAL GENERAL IN MID-LIFE

For people who are General-Nurses, the mid-life switch is the move from the emphasis on the supportive characteristics of the Nurse, towards the General side of their character – ie, moving more towards operating in an authoritative mode. While they were in supportive mode they obtained great fulfilment in being supportive, in receiving instruction, in helping someone else achieve their aims and goals – and in tolerating and putting up with someone else's agenda. But during the mid-life switch period (35 to 42), the General grows more and more into her own authoritativeness, and this is accompanied by the development of a strong feeling of needing to be in control and then of being in control. This process tends to take place at a time when they start to see how bad other people are at being Generals, at running things, at setting standards, and at teaching. Emerging Generals say things like: 'I want to start taking control back in my life, I want to be more independent, I want to make my own decisions, I want to be in charge.'

It's easy to see why the switch from Nurse to General doesn't happen much before the mid-thirties. A potential General aged, say, 25 may *want* to take charge but may not yet have the authority – because of their age, no one has given them the accountability to be in charge. At the same time, their secondary (Nurse) component is still very much to the fore, so they tend to respond emotionally most of the time. At this stage, people don't want to listen to their authoritative side because they're used to being hit with a wave of emotion, which can be very offputting and uncomfortable, especially when they are trying to be authoritative at the same time. Their authoritative side ends up being discounted by all around them, so they have to serve their time, go through the grind of doing somebody else's bidding, having to respond to somebody else's authority.

PERFORMERS AT THE LIFE-CYCLE WATERSHED

Performers, the networkers, the flamboyant people of this world, don't really fit into organisations or teams. They themselves feel like outsiders, although they desperately want to belong. They 'move into', and become more comfortable with, their Performer state – largely because they move further up the organisation as they get older, and so they have more power and (which they value more) greater status. It's a continual process of transition, maturing and emerging – an increasing comfortableness with one's position.

THE SOLIDER BECOMING A PERFORMER

A Performer-Soldier would probably join a company early on in life and then remain extremely loyal to it. He would work hard for the organisation, in a loyal and supportive way – ie, exploring his secondary component. He could suffer rejection because he may not have formally qualified as a professional and, as a result, be looked down upon. But to leave the organisation would be too much of a wrench. As he reaches mid-life, he starts to leave the soldiering behind and begins to want to get more in touch with his Performer and, in particular, his networking and ambassadorial qualities.

At this stage, the lack of respect he's accorded may become a huge source of pain and anguish – it may be so great that he decides to switch companies, to go off and find a different 'army' in which he's accorded some respect. Performers need status – fancy cars, titles, etc – so that (in their own eyes and in reality) they become better ambassadors. Status (not power) is the main motivational force for performers. They often feel they want power but there is a confusion here: they actually want status, but it happens that status and power usually go together.

PEOPLE WHO CAN'T CHANGE

Some people never get in touch with their primary component – they feel, 'I've always done things this way and I'm too old to change my spots.' Deep down, they may be frightened at the prospect of becoming someone different. Getting in touch with the primary component will almost certainly mean that you will at least want to live in a different atmosphere and a different environment, and it may mean that you find you want to change your job and change your partner. People often feel that they need a different set of relationships in order to discover and then nurture their 'new' selves – ie, who they really are.

The Chalkcheese team members: a bit more flesh on the bones

Gail, aged 34, is a General-Nurse – ie, primarily (60 per cent) General with a secondary (40 per cent) Nurse component in her personality. She achieved 3 A' Levels and went on to university to read for (and secure) an excellent degree in business studies. Ambitious and a good administrator, she has been with Chalkcheese all her working career.

Natalie is 42 and a Nurse-General (80 per cent Nurse and 20 per cent General). She got no further than some O' Levels at school, and went on to complete a secretarial course. Natalie had a couple of low-powered local government jobs before leaving work to be with her two children. She resumed work when the children started school, joining Chalkcheese's customer services department, and is now one of its longest serving members.

Patrick, aged 27, is a Performer-General (70 per cent Performer and 30 per cent General). He struggled a little at school and university, but did manage two A' Levels and a third-class degree in social studies. After four different jobs in five years, Patrick joined the Chalkcheese marketing department last year.

Stuart is 48 and a Soldier-General (60 per cent Soldier and 40 per cent General). Two A' Levels secured him a place at a polytechnic where he obtained an accountancy qualification. After polytechnic, Stuart worked successively for a number of the larger accounting practices for ten years, before joining Chalkcheese's accounts department 17 years ago. He has steadily, if unspectacularly, gained promotion within the department, and is now financial controller, in charge of the department's basic number-crunching activities.

HUMAN TECHNOLOGY – A CHECKLIST

■ **Generals** are logical, organised, goal-oriented, decision makers and

69

planners. They are not good with people, and not very instinctive or creative.

- **Nurses** are warm, supportive, emotional and considerate. They have good intuition, particularly about other people, but are disorganised and poor problem solvers.

- **Performers** are visionaries – instinctive and creative. They are volatile and unstructured, but capable of highly original thinking, although they have poor planning and implementation skills.

- **Soldiers** are thorough, cautious and hardworking. They dislike change, and taking command, although they enjoy implementing clear plans and strategies, once they've grasped what's required of them.

- We all have a primary and a secondary component from the Human Technology system – in differing proportions.

- Until about age 35 our lives tend to be motivated by our secondary personality component, but from about 35 to 42 we tend to want to move into our primary component.

4

Identifying Human Technology types in yourself and others

After reading Chapter 3 you probably already have some ideas about how you and your colleagues fit the Human Technology system. When I'm called in as a consultant, what I do is sit down and ask people to tell me a story about what they feel have been significant aspects of their lives from around age 11 onwards. Just listening to people telling you what they've done in their lives, their feelings, aspirations and so on, can give you a lot of information about how they are likely to behave now, and in the future.

Chalkcheese Ltd – the players learn about Human Technology

The think-tank is again in chaos, and Gail is frustrated by the failure of her efforts to organise and plan a progressive approach to devising and selecting a new computer system.

One evening, outside work, she meets Martin C, a management consultant, and describes the situation to him. He suggests that Human Technology could help her understand what makes each of the members of the think-tank tick. If she knew that, she'd be better able to predict how they are going to react, what to expect, the best ways to cure some of the conflict, and how to get the best from them.

Gail: OK, so how do I work out how we all fit into the Human Technology system?

Martin: Well, let's start with you. What would you say is your major behavioural component – how old are you, by the way?

Gail: Thirty-four. I think, probably General.

Martin: What's your educational background?

Gail: I did a business studies degree and then joined the Chalkcheese graduate training programme.

Martin: Can you tell me a little bit about what you see as some of the important events and turning points in your life.

Gail: Do you mean since joining Chalkcheese?

Martin: No, start right back from when you were about 11.

Later, after hearing Gail's story, Martin explains the ins and outs of Human Technology to her, and they agree her dominant trait is that of a General. As to Gail's secondary component, the conversation continues . . .

Martin: Tell me, do you cry easily – or do tears come to your eyes, lumps to your throat?

Gail: Not very often.

Martin: But sometimes?.

Gail: Occasionally, yes.

Martin: Do you get upset easily, do words hurt sometimes?

Gail: Yes, I think I am susceptible to that. I guess it means I have some Nurse characteristics.

Martin: I think that's right. My preliminary feeling is you are about 60 per cent General and 40 per cent Nurse. But although you're predominantly General, from what you've told me about the problems you're having with the think-tank you seem unwilling to admit your drive to take the lead, to be authoritative. With people around your age, I often see this sort of denial. This is all to do with the part of you that wants to be supportive – to go on being supportive, not to take control, and not wanting to deal with confrontation. The trouble is that not having control is going to make you more and more unhappy and discontented.

As well as questioning and discussion as a means of eliciting behavioural information, another valuable information source relies on observation. So before looking at individuals and Human Technology, a good place to begin this chapter is to examine the sometimes illuminating ways that whole countries and national populations can been seen to be part of the system.

Human Technology and national characteristics

In Chapter 2, I mentioned ways in which our society influences the development of our behaviour. We absorb social rules and values from everyone around us while we're growing up, that shape our adult behaviour. Our experiences of having our behaviour measured against the norms of our society give us constant feedback as to the most appropriate, successful, and, at a subconscious level, pleasurable, behaviour. One result of this is the preponderance of certain of the Human Technology types in different countries.

ENGLAND – GENERALS

England is a country of Generals. All English people feel they have a right to express a view and a right to remain an individual. 'An English man's home is his castle', and it matters little whether it's a bed-sit or a mansion.

English cultural roots and traditions nurture the development of the individual rather than the team (for example, the English tend not to excel at team sports). But the individual is expected to conform externally to a whole framework of behavioural 'norms', and only certain sorts of departures from this framework are tolerated and forgiven. The 'great British eccentric' remains a national institution, but it is interesting that such people are either sidelined from mainstream society, or are eccentric only in confined and limited aspects of their behaviour, which we find relatively easy to accept and even feel affection for.

73

England, therefore, tends to foster the development of Generals. People who analyse and ponder before reacting, and shy away from the instinctive reaction, even when hindsight shows that trusting their first instinct would have been the most successful strategy. Generals *always* look before they leap.

All professionals possessing formal qualifications are, by definition, Generals. We respect and support academia and academic qualifications – what you do with them is irrelevant.

When professionals are responsible for founding and running an organisation, what tends to happen is that every part of the organisation is clearly defined and relationships, communication and movement between different parts follow pre-set paths. If you want to work your way up in any organisation, you are given a little group to run. If you do that well, then you are given a bigger group to run, and that is how you make progress. This sort of advancement along academic lines, stage-by-stage, suits Generals well. One-star Generals may stay at the level of the small group – four-star Generals will move up as far and as fast as they can.

JAPAN AND GERMANY – SOLDIERS

The Japanese culture also frowns on the instinctive reaction, and hedges communication with elaborate social rules and rituals. The individual is subsumed into the whole. Homogenous groups (such as the army) are the model for companies and organisations. The group always takes precedence. Each member's creative role is defined as thinking 'What is best for the group? What can I contribute to the team?' Corporate and group goals and culture are clearly spelt out, so individuals have no need to think about how to behave. The culture leads to the development of Soldiers and fosters manufacturing industries and mass production.

When Japanese people join organisations they go through a serious training process to bring them up to speed, and, once in the organisation, they usually remain there for a long time. Both the work ethic and the desire 'to please the powers that be' are extraordinarily strong. There is virtually no questioning of authority (in contrast to the English General's approach of questioning just about everything). But the downside of this (for Japan, but also for, say, Germany, which is a Soldier nation as well) is the country's susceptibility to dictatorships: authority figures often assume cult status.

Another, perhaps more endearing example of Japan as a Soldier country, is the common sight of Japanese tourists in foreign cities, where they usually travel around in groups. And at the head of each group you often see a group leader, carrying a little flag to denote his or her role, and providing the focal point for the group to follow.

THE USA – PERFORMERS

A country of Performers who enjoy putting on a show. Where else would you get Ronald Reagan – a 'B' movie actor (and, to be frank, not a brilliant one at that) playing the role of President. The US people loved Reagan, who in all honesty said, 'But hold on . . . I'm really not sure I know what I'm doing.' Nevertheless the US people responded: 'We know that, but you look great and you put on a great show'.

The US is a country of Performers, who don't like order. In contrast to England, where we form orderly queues, without instruction, people in the US don't know what a queue is! 'What do you mean, queue? I was here first!' Americans tend to progress from one crisis to another because, as Performers, they are always fire-fighting, and fires are always breaking out around them. So when a Performer is in any managerial position (political or corporate), their way of moving forward is always jerky, never smooth.

In England, we are very good at repetition, we are very linear. We are good at repeating what we did last year, or last century. Americans are better in, and need, situations of change, and are more likely to reject tradition than to be bound by it.

POLITICS, NATIONAL LEADERS AND HUMAN TECHNOLOGY

National tendencies show up in politics, and the selection of a political leader. When Ronald Reagan stood down, there were two other candidates, George Bush and Michael Dukakis. Both Bush and Dukakis are Generals and therefore were judged by the American population to be boring and unexciting – they could not put on a show. 'How can we pick one of you two if you don't put on a show?' A Performer has now been restored to the White House in the form of Bill Clinton. He talks well, looks good, plays the saxophone and is a showman.

If you look at England, however, we don't appreciate Performers. We want Generals, people we feel we can trust, people whose behaviour we can predict. Michael Heseltine, for example, is a Performer – flamboyant and charismatic. But when he tried to get elected as leader of the Conservative Party and hence Prime Minister, it became clear that people didn't trust him and, instead, John Major (a General-Soldier) was elected.

Germany, like Japan, is a country of Soldiers. Very loyal, structured, hardworking – very factual. Harmony and the idea of service is important to them, and they need directing. Both countries exhibit a recent history of being carried along in the wake of disastrous leaders. It's hard to conceive that dictators would ever come to power in the UK or America.

75

FRANCE AND ITALY – NURSES

France, Italy and many South American nations are examples of Nurse countries – very unstructured, not particularly stable and tending to install a succession of different governments in quick time. These countries flow through life, not very structured, very emotional. It's very acceptable to express your emotions in these countries, while it isn't acceptable at all in England. The French think the English are very stuffy and boring, while we think they are quite excitable and perhaps not to be trusted because of their emotional rather than structured reaction to life.

You never quite know where Nurse countries' loyalties lie. Their allegiances are often many and varied, and the frequent changes of government are an indicator of this. To take an example, France's political posturing has often been intriguing: occasionally they have presented a communist culture to the outside world as close allies of the former Soviet Union, while now they are at the centre of the European Union. But the day before the Gulf War allies went to war with Iraq following its invasion of Kuwait, and well after the European Union had made its stance crystal clear, there was France, behind everyone's back, endeavouring to negotiate and cut a deal with Iraq.

Conditions for business change all the time – they are probably changing now more quickly than any other time in history. To keep up, we need to deal with external circumstances more skilfully. There isn't the time for decision making that we had hundreds of years ago. We need to be much more expert – and quicker with it. The only way we can do that is to develop and follow our instincts – to rely on them and trust them more. Instinct is the only tool that can give us the speed of decision-making needed to cope with the modern pace of change.

Autobiography

As mentioned at the start of this chapter, the main method of classifying people into types in the Human Technology system is to get them to talk about themselves – to ask questions and to show an interest in their lives.

How much do you actually know about your colleagues? You may see them every working day for seven to eight hours, but do you know how old they are? Where they went to school? How they spend their leisure time? All these are pointers to their Human Technology characteristics.

Action

Encourage staff and colleagues to talk about their lives. Compare notes with others – if you're an authority figure, staff may be reluctant to chat freely about themselves, or may be tempted to paint the picture they think you want to see. The object of this exercise is to find out what people are really like, not to see how well they can role-play the 'ideal staff member'!

You should think about:

- *age*
- *education and career path*
- *social life*
- *family life.*

AGE

Someone in their twenties or early thirties is likely to still be mainly exhibiting their secondary Human Technology characteristic, while someone in their mid-forties onwards is likely to be settled into their primary characteristic. When looking at someone in their mid-thirties to mid-forties, they are likely to be in a period of transition from their secondary to primary component. If they are finding this stressful or difficult, this could be making them hard to deal with, or affecting their performance. If they've been in their present niche for some time, they may no longer find that their role within the organisation satisfies their changing desires.

This kind of dissatisfaction – the square peg in the round hole syndrome – can be a key cause of conflict within a company. We'll look at this problem again in detail in several other parts of this book.

The final thing to note about age is that different types of people move through life at different paces. Soldiers, are very slow-paced. Someone whose secondary type is Soldier, but whose primary type is General, may take a long time to come to terms with the desire to take control, to become a leader. He or she may pass the usual mid-thirties to mid-forties period before experiencing the need for change. On the other hand, Performers tend to move through life at a fast pace. Performer-Generals may be pushing for command long before their peers deem them experienced or skilled enough to take control, leading to a potentially dangerous build-up of frustration and resentment, which can be a source of friction and conflict within the company.

77

EDUCATION AND CAREER PATH

Generals have great respect for academic qualifications. All Generals will have achieved some sort of post-school qualification, and many will have gone on to take work-related training courses, often in their own time.

How much moving around from job to job a person has done is also a relevant consideration. If he or she has stayed within the company, how have their role and responsibilities altered since they started? How does this link with their age, and any transition from secondary to primary characteristics they may have undergone?

A Nurse may tell you that they've moved jobs frequently because they've disliked their colleagues or boss, felt unwelcome or left out. A General might move jobs as each posting allowed him to gain new skills, which, once learned, enabled him to move on to a more powerful position. Performers are the most likely to have fallen out with their colleagues and been asked to leave! But they are also the most likely to have started up their own operations – successfully or unsuccessfully.

SOCIAL LIFE

What people do with their leisure time outside the straight-jacket of the working world can be a useful clue to their personality. Soldiers may spend their time in organised group activities – team sports, helping with youth groups or very regimented organisations such as Guides, Scouts or the Territorial Army. Both Performers and Nurses have a creative side to their personality, which may show itself in creative social activities such as art, languages, music or theatre.

Nurses will also enjoy social activities which involve groups rather than solitude – they get a great deal of pleasure from interacting with people. Performers seek excitement and may take up risky and dangerous hobbies – skiing, parachuting, white-water rafting. Generals don't mind being solitary, or spending long periods without communication. They may prefer intellectual pursuits such as chess or crossword puzzles, which Performers wouldn't attend to long enough to find interesting. I have a client, who is a Performer-Soldier. He has tried so many times to play bridge or scrabble and it's hopeless. He just can't get his head round retaining information -- anything to do with order, remembering cards that have gone before, or remembering vocabulary – he finds it boring. Performers (who are often bad at spelling) have little interest in anything cerebral.

FAMILY LIFE

You are unlikely to find either a male or female Performer as half of a happily-married couple of many years' standing (in which neither partner has ever strayed) with a stable family life. Performers are quite often promiscuous and their partners can expect upheavals and instability. It's a strong person who can put up with the Performer's need to be centre stage, and to receive admiration and applause on a continuing basis.

Chalkcheese Ltd – Gail thinks through Natalie's position

Gail's earlier conversation with Martin C, the management consultant (see page 71), makes her look at her colleagues in the think-tank in a new light. She questions her perceptions of them, her assessment of their abilities, her expectations of them, and her attitudes towards them, as well as theirs towards each other. She identifies the Human Technology types of each one, and considers their behaviour within the context of the think-tank.

Natalie, from customer services, is clearly a Nurse (ie, this is her primary component). Gail realises that Natalie has felt uncomfortable with her position from the first formation of the think-tank – that she dislikes her role as 'representative' of her department, and is unwilling to put herself or her ideas forward, in case they are shot down.

'But', Gail asks herself, 'Why was Natalie selected in the first place? Well, she's popular in a large and disparate department, and gets on well with a lot of different people, doing a very demanding job. The people who work there are constantly under pressure from clients and members of the public complaining and asking awkward questions, always trying to get their orders serviced quickly, and expecting immediate responses. Natalie's reputation as someone who can keep things on an even keel is excellent, and because she's been with the company so long, she really knows about the business and the products. She's expected to know about every part of the operation, and to be informed about every new product as well as the old ones. But she probably doesn't recognise her own value – she certainly doesn't blossom under the treatment Stuart and Patrick give her – Stuart bullies her, Patrick ignores her and even I'm guilty of patronising her! What can I do to make the best use of her abilities? How can I make the others (and myself) appreciate her input – or even include her? How can I get her to make a contribution? How can I persuade her to stay on in the think-tank, and not reveal the problems we're having to the rest of the company?'

79

Asking questions

As well as listening to people's life stories, it's also useful to question them directly about what's important to them in life, their picture of work processes, how they see themselves, and their role in the organisation.

It's not really possible to give you a list of questions with multiple-choice answers – those sorts of lists tend to over-simplify and not to take account of all the various major and minor factors which may be affecting people. But depending on how questions are phrased, and fitted in with discussions, you might find the following 'typical answers' helpful.

ANSWERS TO QUESTIONS WHICH HELP IDENTIFY GENERALS

- I like to have things well organised.
- It's important to have a target to work towards.
- I'm considered good at figures.
- I believe more is achieved with just one person in charge.
- I take my responsibilities seriously.
- Wasting time makes me feel guilty.

- My preferred method of working is to make a list and progress through it.
- I find it easy to state my positions in a way that others can understand.
- All disagreements can be sorted out by rational discussion.
- Talking things through is always useful.
- I like having money and material things.
- I'm not very good at telling jokes.
- People sometimes accuse me of being insensitive.
- If I'm honest, I do not really take risks.
- Inside I feel stressed, but I try not to show it.
- Emotional people make me feel ill at ease.

ANSWERS TO QUESTIONS WHICH HELP IDENTIFY NURSES

- I'm quite disorganised.
- I believe in fate.
- I think people should be more caring towards each other.
- There is no excuse for people to get aggressive.
- I like to get to know people well.
- I think I am a creative person.
- I hate confronting anybody about anything.
- I can feel hurt too easily.
- I feel 'lost' in life a lot.
- I cry so easily.
- I would rather keep my opinions to myself than risk upsetting others.
- I'm the one who usually tries to cool people down in an argument.
- I feel more comfortable with someone else giving directions.
- I feel fulfilled playing the supportive role.
- I need to be liked.
- I meander through life.
- It takes a long time for me to get over being hurt.
- My home is very important to me.

ANSWERS TO QUESTIONS WHICH HELP IDENTIFY PERFORMERS

- I often have inspired ideas.

- I find rules and regulations inhibitive.
- I like to let my imagination run wild occasionally.
- I like to try new things.
- I get bored very easily doing a repetitious task.
- I prefer to leave detailed work to others.
- I sometimes bend the truth, but always in a good cause.
- I often get excited by ideas I have.
- I explode very easily.
- I'm eager to get started on things.
- I like being quite disordered.
- I never mean exactly what I say, or say exactly what I mean.
- My timekeeping could be better.
- I have a good 'gut feel' for when a decision is the right one.
- I wear my heart on my sleeve.
- I don't plan enough for other people's liking.
- I'm quite a happy-go-lucky person.
- I tend to get impatient and bored at meetings.
- I have a large network of contacts.
- I prefer starting things to finishing them.
- I tend not to notice other people's feelings.
- I value status more highly than power.

ANSWERS TO QUESTIONS WHICH HELP IDENTIFY SOLDIERS

- I usually finish what I start.
- Sometimes I get too bogged down in detail.
- I keep my emotions under control.
- I am more loyal than most people.
- I always say exactly what I mean.
- Most things can be viewed in a black or white way.
- I think people often change things needlessly.
- I often need a bit of a push to try something new.
- I like to make things with my hands.
- I am more of a doer than a thinker.
- I like finding out how things work.
- Other people would describe me as a 'consistent' person.

- I tend to have a fixed set of friends.
- I believe in saying exactly what I think rather than going round the houses.
- I don't realise when other people seem to dislike me.
- I want to be part of a team.
- I enjoy being directed.
- I have more patience than most.
- I am more realistic than imaginative.

Because I'm using the Human Technology system all the time, my conclusions tend to come instinctively and very quickly. The best way I think I can add to the lists of responses to questions above, is to talk through a particular case and explain what I was thinking at particular stages.

Identifying who's who

This was a partnership called Flowers & Partners, with seven partners. The partner who originally established the business wanted to leave to do other things. He was not the 'senior partner', as such, because he hadn't worked in the practice for six years, but he did have some authority.

How this original partner was to go about severing his ties with the partnership was a matter of dispute, both between the six remaining partners and the one who wished to leave, and amongst the six themselves. They had tried many different avenues to solve it but failed, and that's when I got involved.

What I tried to start with was identifying who the characters were. It's a bit like a football team: you have to work out who the goalkeeper is, the defenders, the attackers, and so on. Stage one, therefore, is to establish who fits where – working out the make-up of the team. I began by trying to find out who the Generals were, and the first thing I asked was what qualifications each of the partners had.

I met all the partners individually, and asked them to give me a brief history of themselves from age 11 to the present day. An aspect of these sessions is that they are generally extremely therapeutic – people usually enjoy the recounting experience, and rarely need much prompting from me. Accounts can be a bit disjointed sometimes, but a particular aspect I'm looking for is whether they left school early or continued through O' and A' Levels, how they felt in an academic situation, whether they had sufficient determination to push themselves through the academic process – people who have stayed the course and got through this process are Generals, and have the capacity for positions of authority. (The only exception to this is people who stay at university and continue in academia. They don't always have authoritative capability, because it's in the commercial world that you put into practice your authoritativeness by being a leader of other people.)

The seven partners split broadly into three older and four younger partners. Having gone through this interview process, I concluded that all of the junior partners, and two of the three older partners, had been through academia and were Generals, while the other older partner, despite his relative seniority, was not qualified at all. I realised that the latter was a Performer. He was completely right-brained: he had no left-brain capability, so he wasn't any good at planning, no good at structure, he wasn't literate, he wasn't numerate – but he could talk, and he could motivate, be an ambassador, network and sell. He was the primary salesman for the entire business.

As the Performer, this guy was not always appreciated by the other partners who were all Generals. The two eldest were both four-star Generals, one of whom was the partner who wanted to leave, therefore, they were the main combatants in the dispute. The remaining four junior Generals supported one or other of the four-star Generals to varying degrees. None of the younger Generals supported the Performer – they didn't really take him seriously.

During this process of getting to know the participants, I was also looking for evidence of the secondary characteristics of those involved by asking them about their emotions. Questions like whether they cry often, do tears come easily, etc. You can in fact tell from someone's demeanour whether there is an emotional side to them – they tend to be wounded easily saying, eg, 'I was very hurt by such and such'; also, they are often talkative – it's the emotional side of them coming forward.

83

You wouldn't get a feeling of an emotional side when talking, for example, to John Major. He is completely left-brained – a General-Soldier (ie primarily a General, with Soldier as the secondary component of his personality) – so he has no emotional component. Lack of emotionality comes across as a lack of animation, inspiration and passion.

The most common behavioural type I come across is the General with the secondary component of the Nurse – the emotional Generals. There's a creative side to them, they have ideas and behave to an extent instinctively – and with their passion, their ambition and their drive forward, they try to bring about what they want out of life.

The four junior partners were all aged around 35 to 38, so they were in the process of letting go of their secondary component (which for all of them was of a supportive nature), and they were starting to get in touch with their major component.

Of the two four-star Generals, the one who wanted to leave was an emotional General. He was very passionate but also, because he got hurt easily, very defensive. I asked him about the dispute and he said that he got very upset by some of the things that were being said and written, and felt that he was under attack, so he attacked back (and very successfully because he was a very good General). The other four-star General wasn't a Nurse, he was a Soldier, and General-Soldiers are really like very thick-skinned steam-rollers. He was not at all emotionally upset by the dispute – he just thought it was a huge waste of time. Nor could he understand why the others were upset – it was a fact of life and something that needed to be sorted out, not agonised over.

The General-Soldier's factual, as opposed to emotional response, was actually very helpful to me. Once emotions are introduced into a dispute it quadruples the amount of time it's going to take to solve anything, because you have to defuse all the emotion and get that out of the way before you are able to look at the facts of the matter and then at the solutions.

Compare and contrast

We've talked about a method for categorising personalities, using the Human Technology system But you already do this yourselves, to some extent. We constantly receive information from the world around us about people and situations, and people's behaviour in those situations. All of us have devised some personal methods of dealing with that mass of information. We rate people into categories according to certain sorts of traits – honesty, intelligence, thrift, kindness, etc, and we ascribe values to them. These traits can be grouped into three main classes:

- **Evaluation**: how good/bad is a person? How much do we like/dislike them?

- **Activity**: to what extent is a person active/passive, leader/follower?

- **Potency**: how strong/weak is this person? How clever/stupid?

There are four problems with systems of categorising people:

- **Differences in labelling**: We don't all use the same labels to mean the same thing. I might say, 'John is intelligent', and mean that he's quick to pick up new ideas. You might disagree, because he's got no academic qualifications – your definition of 'intelligent'.

- **Different experiences**: We don't all necessarily have the same experiences of other people. John's sparky performance when working with me might lead me to label him 'intelligent', but if he finds you daunting and overpowering, he's more likely to make mistakes and less likely to volunteer ideas or solutions. As a result, you're unlikely to think of him as intelligent

- **Different scales of values**: Each of us places a different value on the traits we perceive in others, making them more or less important in the way we evaluate the whole person. For example, I might place a high value on the trait of 'intelligence', and consider that more important in a person than 'warmth' or 'flexibility'. If you think the latter two qualities are essential in a colleague, and rate John low on both, you might still evaluate him more poorly than I would, even if we agree that he rates high on intelligence.

■ **Assumptions of connections**: This can lead to both positive and negative reinforcement of our evaluations. For example, if you place a positive value on a trait such as 'intelligence', and group it together with other traits such as 'organisation' and 'good forward planning', you might be tempted to rate John high on the latter two traits, just because you think he rates high on the former. Conversely, if you place a negative value on 'intelligence', you might tend to attribute such traits as 'intellectual arrogance' and 'elitism' to John.

So, when *actively* thinking about categorising people for Human Technology purposes, as opposed to passive (unconscious) characterisation, which we do all the time, we need to cross-check our ideas with those of others, and to beware of letting our personal biases prejudice us towards a person.

85

IDENTIFYING HUMAN TECHNOLOGY TYPES IN YOURSELF AND OTHERS – A CHECKLIST

■ Get people to tell you about their lives and themselves – what they've done, where they've been, what they like and dislike are all clues to their personality.

■ Find out about their age, education, career path, social life, and family life.

■ For most people, transition from secondary component to primary component takes place between the ages of 35 and 42. Take this into account when working out how they fit into the Human Technology system.

■ Ask people direct questions about work practices, ethics, styles, and how they see their roles, strengths and weaknesses – and **listen** to their answers.

5

Incompatibility and mismatches

Chalkcheese Ltd – Gail tries to make peace

The day after her meeting with Martin C, the management consultant, Gail asks Natalie to join her for lunch, and requests her not to speak to her head of department about withdrawing from the think-tank until they've talked. Natalie agrees to come, but clearly feels very nervous and upset, and dreads the prospect of more anger and rudeness.

Gail: I'm really sorry that you want to withdraw from the think-tank. I realise that events have been very confused, and that people haven't been very pleasant to each other. But I've had some ideas about how to improve things, and I'd really like you to think about them before you decide to go.

Natalie: Well, I suppose . . .

Gail: Listen, first of all, let me tell you all about 'Human Technology' . . .

. . . Half an hour later

Gail: . . . so you see, our problem as a group is that we all have unrealistic expectations of each other. We've all got ideas about what roles we're each supposed to play, and when the others don't read the right scripts, we get upset!

Natalie: I see what you mean, but what can we do about it?

Gail: Instead of trying to make each of us behave in the same way, we should use the different strengths and abilities we each have for the most appropriate jobs. Stuart has a lot of seniority in the company, and although he's not someone who will make things happen – an innovator – he'll be the right person to collect all the departmental information. He can go on bullying people until they fill in our questionnaire, just to get rid of him!

Natalie: I see – and you can design the questionnaire, because you've already started to think about it, and have an idea of what's going on in all the different parts of the business.

Gail: Yes. But I want your help. You already have a lot of knowledge about how the different departments interact, because customer services deals with everyone – and you end up sorting out the mess when things go wrong!

Natalie: That sounds fine, and I'll be happy to help with that. But I can't bear any more of those meetings where Stuart, Patrick and you just yell at each other!

Gail: No, we have to stop that happening. It's wasteful, and it won't do any of us any good. So I want us to think about how to introduce the ideas of Human Technology to the others, and how to get them to take up roles that are complementary instead of conflicting.

Square pegs in round holes

Some people just don't seem to fit in, and this chapter discusses the problem, especially in relation to organisations and teamwork. The causes of incompatibility and mismatches are examined, and what can be done using the Human Technology system to ensure that your team operates as smoothly and effectively as possible.

Gail, in the Chalkcheese episode above, is taking the first steps towards using Human Technology. She's starting to consider how the *people* components in the think-tank *machine* work, how they function, how they are connected, and how to get each part functioning maximally.

87

This procedure is:

- **Step 1**: identify individual personalities.
- **Step 2**: look at the roles they are filling – are you using the right person for the job? What *is* the job?
- **Step 3**: is one person preventing another from doing his or her job properly?
- **Step 4**: can you change the role, the connections, or the mechanism to help that person to perform optimally? If not, is there a way to isolate the problem person so that they can still be useful?
- **Step 5**: if you can't fit the person to the role, or into the network of roles and people you have, or set them up on their own, but still with an umbilical cord into the organisation, then you have to accept that he or she really has no function in the organisation.

DEFINING ROLES

Action

Consider the main purpose of your job/function/role.

List the three top priorities that contribute to you achieving this purpose:

1 _____

2 _____

3 _____

Describe the personal changes you need to undergo to help fulfil the above purpose/priorities:

_____

_____

_____

_____

The 'sink or swim' syndrome is not uncommon. It's easy to give someone a job title, put them into a department or team, vaguely outline some responsibilities, then to let them get on with it, without you or them ever defining what the job role really is. What are your expectations, what are theirs? Is the person, for example:

- a leader
- an innovator
- a systems designer
- a fulfiller
- a supporter
- a communicator
- a catalyst
- a technician
- a teacher
- a reporter
- a disciplinarian
- a mediator
- a driving force
- a moderating influence?

These roles are not mutually exclusive – one person can fulfil several at the same time, or perform in different roles in different situations. Conflict arises when:

- outside perceptions of the roles associated with the job differ from those of the person doing the job;
- different people within the organisation see different roles associated with the job;
- the person doing the job feels uncomfortable with some roles, or inadequate;
- the person doing the job tries to take on additional roles which others don't associate with that position;
- requirements of different roles clash;
- colleagues, staff or managers feel doubt about the person's ability to fulfil the requirements of their role(s).

I have a female client, aged 42, who is managing director of a quite substantial (£40 million turnover per annum) family-owned business. She has two sisters and four brothers, and two of the brothers are older than her. The main struggle she faced was that her brothers and one of her sisters had different priorities to her concerning 'family first or business first'. They considered the family should always come first, whereas she generally preferred to give priority to the business.

I sat down with her and we drew up a chart (see Figure 5.1) covering all the different roles she performs – the different hats she wears. She's a sibling, the MD, a shareholder, a wife, a mother and a friend – and we went through each, scoring out of ten how effectively she felt she was performing in these different roles.

On a scale of 0 to 10 in each case, as a wife she gave herself 8, as a mother 9, as a friend 8, as a sibling 2, as an MD 8, and as a shareholder 7. Adding this all up, she rated herself 42/60 – ie, she was giving 70 per cent of her whole self in relation to these roles. We never give 100 per cent on anything but, especially as a sibling, she realised she was not offering very much and appreciated the seriousness of this in the context of a family business in which the siblings were also her fellow directors and equity shareholders. Following this exercise – a helpful approach to analysing what's going on – the message became clear that she needed to upgrade the attention and effort she put into performing this sibling role.

89

Roles and Human Technology

The preceding chapters will have given you an idea about what sort of roles the different types within the Human Technology system are suited to. Let's look at them in more detail.

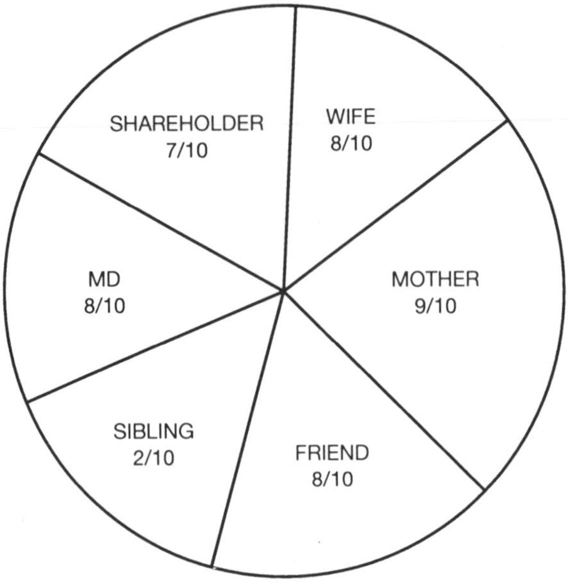

Fig. 5.1 Self-scoring in different roles

PERFORMERS – GOOD INNOVATORS, POOR PLANNERS, DREADFUL IMPLEMENTERS

Because they are such inconsistent, Will-o'-the-wisp butterflies, it's no good putting Performers into, say, a production job where they are expected to work like everyone else, get in on time, follow the traditions, get things done the way they've always been done. It's a waste of a Performer's particular abilities, but even more important, he'll disrupt and unsettle the rest of your 'doers'. Imposing structure on a Performer results in him feeling trapped and, in due course, will lead to an explosion. Yet, if you let him get away with arriving late, changing work patterns and hopping from task to task in search of something he finds interesting and challenging, you'll stir up resentment against both him – for getting away with it – and yourself, for letting him!

Trying to bring him into line, to get him to perform within the confines of the role, will result in friction, rows, and face-to-face unpleasantness. At best, your Performer will up and leave. At worst, you suffer an unpleasant, divisive atmosphere, with other staff taking sides, perhaps forming allegiances and cliques, ruining the cohesiveness of your former smooth-running team.

You wouldn't let a Performer near an operation of this sort *unless* you wanted change. If you're questioning, 'Are we doing the right thing? Are we doing it the right way? Should we be doing this at all?', then you might want to introduce a Performer (but with his role clearly defined, for his sake, your sake and the sake of the 'doers' he'll come into contact with) as that of 'innovator', 'ideas-merchant', or 'catalyst'.

A charismatic, strong Performer can be a magnetic, overwhelming leader. Performers are agents of change. One of their skills is to identify and understand the need for change (they recognise stagnation instinctively), but they may not always be able to formulate a clear plan about what form the change should take. A Performer feels that part of his duty as a leader is to bring about change, and sometimes this can develop into almost a mission.

Because Performers rarely perceive risk, most of their ideas are on a grand scale – the world can be their oyster. Things can go wrong, but there is often magic about the way they can repeatedly dig themselves out of holes and end up, once again, delivering the goods.

If you try and let a Performer loose in the 'innovator' role, you have to be prepared to trust his instincts – and yours. Surround and support him with people who'll investigate and check out even the wildest notions, not instantly react with, 'That's brilliant, let's do it', or alternatively, 'That won't work, we can't do that.'

91

Performers with other types

Performers are not team players – they are always mavericks. Generals and Soldiers (both predominantly left-brain, logical, problem-solving personalities) live by order and regimen, in contrast to right-brain Performers and Nurses. Generals and Soldiers are suspicious of the Performer in the innovator role. They don't like change anyway, and distrust the idea of change for it's own sake. But they like him even less in a support or production-oriented role – they have no patience or understanding of his basic incapacity to fit in, knuckle down and get on. They label him 'lazy' or 'disruptive'.

Performers act like very receptive antennae who can pick up signals from all around themselves. They may not know what the signals mean or what to do with them, but they are excellent at picking up the information. This is why the rest of the team around them are so important. Performers need to be 'debriefed' and to have the signals they collect interpreted. Once this has been done, the General can plan a strategy to move forward, making the most of the information gathered by the Performer.

It is important to set up a support structure of people whom the Performer likes and trusts. Remember that Performers like to be liked – they're sociable and emotional people. Since they're unlikely to come back from trawling trips with neat reports, lists of names to follow up and clear strategies to pursue, there has to be someone there for him to tell about it – someone with enough experience to tease out all the details, enough knowledge to use the information effectively – passing it on to where it will be of the most use, and at the same time, giving the Performer the acknowledgement and encouragement which he needs and on which he thrives.

Perhaps one of the most important things to think about when trying to establish organisational roles for Performers is what you, and the rest of the company, *don't* expect from them. If you make it clear – in your own mind, in the Performer's mind and in those of his staff, colleagues and managers – that, for example, you expect him to go out and pursue new business, to chat up new clients, to put out feelers into new markets, and that you *don't* therefore expect him to attend department meetings, fill in report forms, take on a share of staff training, and so on, then you reduce the likelihood of making the Performer feel trapped and you reduce the potential for conflict.

It's interesting that many successful entrepreneurs who are notorious for wearing out managers and senior staff at speed – they can't keep up, or put up, with the 'great man' – often have a long-serving dedicated secretary or assistant who has 'been beside them from the start'. This person can often act as memory bank, communication channel, planner, interpreter and shield, and one can't imagine the Performer surviving without them.

A useful analogy here is to see the key to the success of a Performer in the form of a maypole around which they can float. The function of this maypole is to help structure their activities and the results of their efforts. A General who has – as well as her logical and problem-solving primary component – a lot of 'support' characteristics, will be suited to this role.

From a day-to-day support perspective, Soldiers get on best with Performers because Soldiers do not get thrown off balance or frightened by the Performer. But Nurses tend not to be able to relate well to Performers. This is because a Performer's central core is raw emotion which Nurses, who are also emotional, simply find too disruptive and too threatening.

Groups of Performers have to be handled carefully. It would be madness to bring together all those creative, disorganised, individualists, and expect them to fall into a coherent team. Performers need their own personal stage, their own limelight, and giving each his own area/client list and encouraging the kind of organised competition that can only result in benefits for the company, will almost certainly turn out to be a successful strategy.

GENERALS – GOOD PLANNERS AND PROBLEM SOLVERS, POLITICAL AND MANIPULATIVE

Generals, like Performers, are leaders rather than followers, but with a completely different style. Generals (particularly strong ones – the four-star Generals) need to take control, to take on power and responsibility. If held back, especially by people whom they perceive as incompetent or disorganised, they become extremely frustrated and unhappy. If they don't receive the respect and rewards they feel are their due, they become restless. Their drive to succeed is constantly nagging at them, telling them they haven't got far enough, haven't achieved enough. Because Generals tend to be logical, efficient and systematic, they can create havoc within a team or organisation in their struggle to attain their desired position. They may try to shift the balance of power, to divide staff loyalties to themselves, to undermine senior management, and at the last, to leave the organisation taking with them inside information and expertise which they can offer to a competitive organisation prepared to supply them with the power they crave. (We return to the subject of power games and authority in Chapter 7.)

Generals can function in support roles, if they see these as leading on to the eventual assumption of authority. Generals are nothing if not logical – explain to one that keeping their project going requires them to back up, shield and control the loose cannon which is its figurehead, and this will make perfect sense. However they will want to see where this is leading, and while they are happy to see themselves as 'the power behind the throne', they won't want to get trapped into the role of permanent back-room boy.

93

Coming up with innovative ideas is not something to look to Generals for, although they can be the best people, once convinced of the value of an innovation, to take responsibility for its implementation. They'll be happy to move people, equipment and money around, and to set up new systems. Getting rid of the old ways will be harder for them, and unless they've been convinced of the logic behind a change in policy or goal, they are more likely to fight than support it.

Generals make thorough but tough trainers. They have poor people skills and are impatient with slow learners – and, importantly, with those who question their training. They are not good at soothing wounded feelings, calming insecurities, or communicating at a personal level. This means that they have flaws as trouble-shooters. You might send a General in to sort out a mess – a department or project in crisis – but if the problems are emotion and personality-based, they may well make things worse rather than improve them. It may even be impossible for them to recognise what the causes of the conflict are. This is less so for the emotional General – the General who can call on his or her secondary

Nurse component for an instinctive empathy with the people involved in the situation. They'll be very good at reorganisation, thinking up strategies and logical solutions – taking a crisis and ruthlessly deciding what to scrap and what to concentrate on. Generals are good at discipline – prepared to sack those they perceive as troublemakers, lazy, or redundant, although emotional Generals may agonise over such decisions, their logical and emotional sides in internal conflict.

Generals with other types

Generals really come to the fore when there is a clear battle to be fought, and they can establish an objective that they want to 'win'. Generals' relations with others tend to be somewhat manipulative – in the battle to come they need to know whose side each person is on, and are always aware of the risks should someone change sides. They play their cards close to their chests, and others may find them unapproachable, hard to get to know, and somewhat compartmentalised.

Soldiers and Generals, as the names suggest, work well together – Soldiers relish the clear instructions, organised approach and authoritarian stance of Generals. However a company consisting only of Soldiers and Generals could be very rigid, blinkered and inflexible. Generals working with Nurses run the risk of trampling on their sensibilities, and of being too authoritarian to get the benefit of their creative and intuitive abilities.

The relationship between groups of Generals depends on whether or not they all agree on their relative places in the hierarchy. Things are OK if each one accepts his or her position:

'I'm a one-star General, you're a three-star General: I don't know as much as you do, and you've got more fighting power than me, so I'll accept your authority.'

'I'm a General and you're a General: we've each got command of a group, and we're each implementing our parts of an agreed strategy in order to win the common battle.'

But if there's a power struggle, with less powerful Generals trying to gain more power and influence, or disagreement over areas of responsibility, with two or more Generals tussling to gain control, then internal conflict is the result. Generals are logical and good problem solvers, so if they can be made to see how damaging their power struggle is, they can find ways to deal with it. In the meantime, the company may have suffered terrible wounds that will take a long time to heal.

Chalkcheese Ltd – the General's strategy

Gail and Natalie draw up a detailed questionnaire (about current computer use, staffing, information and reporting needs, etc) for each Chalkcheese department. Gail also telephones the computer expert, Cliff Thompson from Tecsol. She explains that she and the others hadn't expected him at the meeting the other day, so they weren't fully prepared for him. She tells him about the idea of collecting more information from the other departments, and he is immediately enthusiastic, and makes several useful suggestions for the questionnaire. Gail also agrees a fee structure with him, and they decide how to proceed next. When she comes off the phone she has a distinct sense of Cliff's relief at having a clear plan to follow!

Her next step is to tackle Stuart, who is still furious with Patrick and ready to go to the board of directors and suggest that the think-tank be disbanded.

We talked about the relationships between Generals and Performers earlier in this chapter – how their leadership styles differ, and the trouble they find with each other in 'support' roles. This is made very clear in the case of Flowers and Partners, first discussed in Chapter 4 (pages 82–84). Let's look in more detail at the interaction between the different Human Technology types in this situation, and see how the incompatibility and mismatches were identified and dealt with.

95

Flowers & Partners – Generals and Performers

To recap, in this case there were seven partners – the founding partner, (an emotional General) who wanted to leave the partnership, two senior partners who joined very soon after the partnership was founded, and four junior partners (all emotional Generals). The two senior partners represented the rest of the partners in the confrontation that took place with the founding partner over his leaving plans, but, in addition, they had some difficulty as regards their relationship with each other. This is the aspect of the problem I want to concentrate on here.

One of the two senior partners was a Performer-Soldier – ie, his dominant characteristic was that of Performer and his secondary component was Soldier. In his early years he was very happy to be the Soldier, and worked very hard. He was the only member of the partnership governing board who was not qualified: to go through academia you have to have left-brain qualities. A Soldier, who is a support element, may well have struggled through secondary education (often tending to take up one of the secondary trades – plumber, carpenter, electrician, etc), but is very unlikely to have gone on to higher education where, to succeed, you almost inevitably have to be a General. So although a senior partner, this individual was in large part a Soldier – not qualified, which, in the context of a professional practice in which everyone else had academic qualifications, was a source of insecurity for him.

The secondary component of the other senior partner in the duo was also Soldier, but his primary component was that of a General – ie, a General-Soldier. By the time I met them, both partners were in their mid-40s and had moved into their primary components (*see 'Human Technology and the life cycle' in Chapter 3, page 65*). So there was competition between the Performer, who wanted status, and the General, who wanted power. The Performer-Soldier was quite an emotional character, who was articulate but not consistent. In his early days with the partnership he used to be reliable, very solid, and an extremely valuable member of the junior staff – but as he matured and gained seniority he used more of his emotional qualities of leadership and, at the same time, found himself more and more out of sync with his colleagues who were all Generals. As a result he came to feel isolated, hurt and unappreciated.

The General-Soldier, on the other hand, had no emotion in him whatsoever, was extremely thick-skinned and very much like a steamroller. As such, he used to ride rough-shod over the other senior partner's feelings and was confident in knowing what his own responsibilities, capabilities and role amounted to. The Performer was less sure-footed – he was a salesman but, with the onset of the recession, he had nothing to sell and no one to sell to. Most of the other professionals in the partnership – the Generals – were able to perform ongoing duties for established clients, securing income for the business. But the Performer felt redundant and even contemplated moving, because it was unclear what he could contribute in a recession (which, with no new business around, was really not very much). Performers in these conditions tend to suffer, and their problem is exacerbated because they are emotional people, subject to depression: they can lose all the motivation and enthusiasm that in other circumstances makes them so valuable to the group.

Towards a solution
So having talked to everyone involved, thought through what was going on and arrived at my analysis, I explained and discussed my conclusions with those involved. First, I explained at great length and in great detail my thoughts on the dynamics of the relationship to the General-Soldier – the qualities that someone like his co-senior partner, a Performer-Soldier, brings to the organisation, and also the fears and concerns they suffer. I wasn't surprised to find that this analysis was a revelation as far as the General-Soldier was concerned – being completely left brain and linear in his thinking, he was more or less oblivious to the hurts, fears or concerns of anybody else. His other partners – for the most part General-Nurses, and therefore with an emotional perspective to their personalities – were worried about the situation of the business at this time and what was going to happen. In fact, the General-Soldier's thick-skinned, single-minded, dogged approach, although lacking sensitivity, actually turned out to be

a source of strength for the partnership at this particular time, and helped see it through a difficult period.

When I explained to the General-Soldier the detrimental, destructive effect that his methodology was having on his opposite half – his fellow senior partner, the Performer-Soldier – he was taken aback, surprised, but also immediately sympathetic and concerned. He had never intended to cause distress or to be destructive: he had just wanted to implement the game plan as he saw it. So to be told he was causing fear and wounding colleagues was distressing and alarming. It would have been possible for the General-Soldier to have dismissed the possibility of changing his behaviour – 'this is what I am and what you see is what you get' could have been his response. But luckily he did realise that outside of his blinkered vision, all was not well.

I then undertook the same exercise with the other partner – the Performer-Soldier – explaining to him that this is the way General-Soldiers are: steamrollering, thick-skinned, lacking in subtlety. I told him: 'You, as a Performer-Soldier on the other hand, are trying to be subtle and trying to dilute the pain brought on by the other senior partner's steamroller approach, by hinting that you are not happy with the situation, but your hints are going over his head.' The natural response from the Performer-Soldier, and the only way for him to express distress was to get angry or emotional, but he tried very hard to suppress this because he felt it would make him look silly and encourage people to look down on him. Because he wasn't a General, he couldn't be lucid in his pain and distress, he couldn't intellectualise and think through the problem – all he could potentially do was to let the pain explode out, probably at the wrong time and in the company of the wrong people.

Once I'd explained to the two senior partners their traits, key personality characteristics and particular skills, they developed an appreciation of each other. They appreciated also that they were 'locked in' and that it was unlikely that either of them could leave because of the financial burdens this would create for the individuals and the remaining partners (after the founding partner, they owned the largest equity participations in the partnership). So they both acknowledged that they needed to learn to work with each other and, as the two senior partners, to drive the practice forward out of recession: they needed to work out ways in which they could *use* each other – use the strengths of the other and accommodate their potential weaknesses.

Prior to this 'awakening', the way the partners had approached their roles was largely based on a hazy, undefined idea about sharing – they shared decision making and important ambassadorial and administrative jobs within the day-to-day operations of the partnership – because they thought this was the best way to demonstrate the mutual support and equilibrium that was expected to exist between the two of them. In fact this idea of sharing was entirely inappropriate. For example, the General-Soldier – the steamroller man – had few skills when it came to talking to staff; he was factual, to the point, but often quite bruising and

97

insensitive. The Performer-Soldier, on the other hand, was surrounded by a sort of atmosphere of empathy and, along with some grandeur, was reckoned by staff to have a heart of gold and (provided he was not in a down mood) was thus able to handle human resource issues in the partnership in a way that didn't upset people.

So, with the two senior partners I looked at the roles and responsibilities that added up to a sort of joint job description for them both. We looked at ways of defining their roles so that, instead of sharing them all equally, they apportioned different roles and responsibilities in a way that played to their individual strengths. The Performer-Soldier would concentrate on anything to do with marketing, PR, advertising, selling, networking, striking out in new directions – ie, put more generally, questions that centred on the partnership's external functioning. The General-Soldier would concentrate on the partnership's internal operations, its efficiency and its forward planning.

This whole process took the best part of a year, but at the end of it the partners understood each other's characteristics, strengths, weaknesses, and more especially they found themselves able to express a lot of aspects of the hurt and pain they had caused each other across the 24 years of their working relationship. They healed wounds from the past, they found a new way of working with each other which they had not dreamed to be possible, the retiring partner left on amicable terms with his former colleagues, and the partnership is now driving itself out of recession under stronger, more effective and more fulfilled leadership.

> **When we truly co-operate, everyone's life is fulfilled.**

So **definition** is a key point here – definition of:

- roles
- responsibilities
- accountability.

NURSES – GOOD SUPPORTERS, POOR PROBLEM SOLVERS, DREADFUL DECISION MAKERS

Nurses are receptive to what's going on, and they are also instinctive. But they don't function as agents of change – they can't bring about change in the way Performers do, through their power and clout. But Nurses do tune into change and often have a keen sense of what is happening. Of the support types, they are much more accepting of change than Soldiers, and can be of great assistance to a group or organisation facing change, as they can help to nurture individuals and teams through what is often a painful process – communicating in words and on a level that others can recognise and accept.

Nurses are not natural leaders. They don't like taking charge, taking responsibility for planning and decision making. They can act as managers of small groups – they make good trainers, interested in and proud of the development of others under their eye. They are ready to invest time in helping others to achieve their goals, and will work hard to ensure the team meets corporate goals. Nurses are also successful as conduits of information – making sure that people's ideas and feelings get transmitted to all concerned.

In the role of 'trouble-shooter' Nurses have both skills and shortfalls which are the opposite to those of Generals in this role. They are poor at getting rid of problems requiring, say, strict discipline, or reorganisation, but great at settling insecurity, patching up quarrels, getting rid of rivalry, re-instating communication. They are good mediators at a person-to-person level, because they'll take the trouble to listen to everyone's point of view. Nurses are easily bullied and cowed, however, and tend to be insecure about their abilities so are unlikely to stand up to challenges, or to face up to rows.

On the other hand, Nurses will generally defend their team with intense vigour. While their emotional preponderance can either be an enormous asset or a tremendous liability – it depends on whether they are in control of their emotions or are controlled by them – they care about their group, team or company and will fight for it with all they've got.

Nurses with other types

Generals and Performers can find Nurses ideal in a support role. Generals particularly can benefit from a Nurse's creative input, and, if they learn to trust and use her instinctive qualities, can gain an edge which the unemotional General alone fails to find. Nurses can be good back-ups to Performers too, but if neither of them contain any left-brain elements of logic and problem solving, then the partnership or team can become dangerously disorganised. Both Generals and Performers can be guilty of undervaluing the Nurse – either by not recognising her important contributions or by taking them for granted.

Groups formed solely of Nurses and Soldiers suffer from a lack of leadership, and may work fine at a low level in business, but will not be dynamic or able to run their own affairs. Nurses lack the confidence in themselves to bring about change, even when they can see the need or instinctively feel that it's time for change. Soldiers are unlikely to value

99

Nurses: they distrust their emotional behaviour and, as a result, can be hurtful and dismissive.

SOLDIERS – GOOD 'DOERS', POOR PLANNERS, DREADFUL INNOVATORS

Soldiers are good people to have on your team when you want to get things done. Their thorough, careful, hard-working, reliable approach make them the ideal back-up to a General, who will be prepared to give them clear directions, as well as to define and delimit their roles. Working with Performers, Soldiers are likely to get confused. They'll hate the changes of direction, the decisions taken on instinct, the absence of planning and strategy. Their insecurity can lead to their withdrawal from active participation in team planning and discussions – the 'I just do my job' mentality.

Soldiers find it hard to accept change – any change is for the worse in their minds. But if they must accept change, they take to it more easily if it's presented to them as a *fait accompli*, but with an underpinning of logic and fact that they can grasp. Once they've 'got their minds around' the new system, goal or strategy, they'll be just as tenacious and stubborn in its pursuit as they were of the old ways, so they are very unsuited to any role which requires flexibility.

Soldiers like to progress one project at a time – to 'get the job done'. Because of this, they often become very skilled at their specialist area, and are very productive. While it's important to recognise and reward this, in our 'vertically organised' companies it's easy to include promotion as part of the reward, thus moving the Soldier further and further away from the structured 'doing' role in which he shone, and loading him with other responsibilities. These may be confusing or distressing to her. It's hard to combine the mentality of 'one job at a time – always finish what you start', with the role of reacting quickly to changes in outside conditions, rescheduling, reprioritising and re-organising.

Nevertheless, Soldiers can make good managers, so long as they are not moved too far away from their own areas of expertise, and so long as they are buffered from the immediate consequences of change by a senior manager they respect and trust, who can think through the consequences of change and present them with clear instructions to follow and implement. They enjoy a harmonious and happy team, but will be the last to pick up 'vibes' from discontented, insecure or unhappy staff. The first the Soldier will know of emotional upheavals or potential personality conflicts is when the whole office blows up in his face, or he confronts a mass mutiny!

Soldiers are good at taking discipline themselves, and at working in a disciplined way – and they will expect the same of others. They see no problem in obeying rules, getting in on time, concentrating on the job in hand, and are scornful and resentful of those whose work patterns are different. Their idea of disciplining others can be heavy-handed and insensitive.

Often Soldiers are labelled as lazy. But this generally relates to them not knowing what to do next, and does not indicate a lack of willingness or application.

Soldiers with other types

As we discussed earlier, Soldiers and Nurses can work well together in teams, but need direction, and will not be dynamic without some leadership input. Soldiers function well under Generals but dislike working for Performers, whose volatility they distrust and are confused by. Soldiers placed in leadership roles – in charge of Generals or Performers – will feel very uncomfortable. Soldiers are not natural leaders, and the two leadership types will undermine and run rings around them. The Soldiers' reaction might be to withdraw from decision making and any action which could open them up to challenge, or to try to curb and hem in the potential trouble-maker. Soldiers make stolid managers, but, when in charge of Nurses, they are unlikely to communicate well, and can be insensitive to emotional currents and issues.

Soldiers and Nurses are basically people who feel fulfilled in a support position. Hospitals are primarily staffed by these types, who feel genuine fulfilment in providing support, emotionally and practically. Unsurprisingly, armies are full of 'Soldiers': literally the soldiers of the world who join armies where they are told what to do, when to do it and how to do it. The only requirement as far as they are concerned is to deliver. They don't have to take the initiative, they are not asked to be responsible, they are not asked to make decisions, or to direct others. You could look upon that as a liability, but to Soldiers it's precisely what they do best and what makes them feel most fulfilled.

Unfortunately both support types (ie, Nurses and Soldiers) are taken advantage of: people use the fact that these personalities feel fulfilled in providing service, so when it comes to rewarding them financially, they are very low on the list. For the British Army or British Health Service workers to go on strike is very rare, because they are mainly populated by Soldiers and Nurses who usually shy away from decision making and do not feel capable of taking control of situations.

> **In ancient China the medical profession was only rewarded when people were well. They got paid when the patient was in a good condition. When the patient wasn't well the doctors weren't paid because they obviously weren't doing their job. So, the consciousness of the medical profession was maintenance of well-being and good health. The doctors were rewarded not for initiative but for maintenance, which is a complete reversal of current thinking.**

Change

Paradoxically, the only constant in life is change, and the degree of comfort and ease we have during life is a reflection of our ability to manage change (a subject that is discussed in detail in Chapter 6). Business is constantly changing as the outside world changes; customers and products change; people come and go; people's levels of experience change, they acquire more responsibility and seniority; their home and family circumstances change, affecting their behaviour and performance at work.

This constant change can be the major cause of incompatibilities and mismatches. Why does someone who's done a job well for many years suddenly seem to perform less well? He could be suffering the effects of a change over which he has no control such as the introduction of a new team member whom he finds challenging or difficult. Or he could be undergoing a change from his minor to his major personality component – feeling uncomfortable and unfulfilled in the role he plays within the business. Change will alter your carefully selected team from one which has all the components necessary to take the business forward or to see through the project it was set up for, to one totally unsuited to coping with current circumstances.

Human Technology is *dynamic*, not *static*. People change, circumstances change, targets and systems change. You can't think about Human Technology once, put a few ideas in place and then leave it for review in a year's time. You have to be constantly working at it, using some of the tools I talk about in the next chapter – communication, rhythm and goal setting.

INCOMPATIBILITY AND MISMATCHES – A CHECKLIST

■ Different jobs involve different roles – clarify what these are for yourself, the person involved and his or her colleagues.

- Some human technology types are better in certain roles than others. Try and ensure that the optimum role is allocated to each type.

- Performers make good innovators, ambassadors, salespeople and networkers.

- Generals make good problem-solvers, planners, administrators.

- Nurses make good supporters, trainers, carers.

- Soldiers make good fulfillers, doers, back-up.

- People go through change, companies go through change, the world goes through change. Human Technology is about making sure that the human elements in a team are helped to cope with change rather than being undermined by it.

6

Influencing reactions in others

Chalkcheese Ltd – the General and the Soldier

Gail is trying to defuse tensions between the members of the think-tank, and to prevent the conflict from spreading and becoming obvious to the rest of the company. Her next move is to talk to Stuart, the Soldier. She fixes an appointment to see him.

Gail: Stuart, thanks for seeing me. I've been doing some work on the computer planning since the think-tank meeting, and I'd like to tell you about it – and to ask for your help.

Stuart: I'm not sure we can carry on with the think-tank at all – Patrick has completely messed it up. And as for his *golfing pal* . . .!

Gail: I know Patrick can go off on a bit of a tangent. But he has had some good ideas. I think his problem is that he's just not the kind of person to sit at a desk, plan, draw up forms and reports and analyse the results. I think that's more in the line of you and I.

Stuart: You're right there! Lazy young so-and-so!

Gail: Oh no, I don't think he's lazy at all! I think he'd work very hard at a project he cared about and in a role that he was interested in. But with *our* project at a 'paperwork' stage, he's not the best person to take care of it.

Stuart: So you think we should continue the think-tank without him?

Gail: No, I think we'll need him in the future. He originally sold us on the idea of going for a major change, and I think his skill is going to be selling our decision to the heads of department, and the Board!

Stuart: So what is it you want *me* to do?

Gail: This is the questionnaire I've drawn up, with the help of Natalie and Cliff Thompson, the computer expert from Tecsol. If we can get all the heads of department to fill it in thoroughly and quickly, it will mean Cliff has a clear brief as to what's wanted. It's quite long and detailed as you can see – more of a future planning document than a simple questionnaire. I'm going to take it round to each head of department now, but I'd like you to follow it up and make sure they all get it back to us by the deadline. Then I think you and I should do a detailed analysis and integration of them all.

We've looked at how to identify different types of people within the Human Technology system, and which types are best suited to which roles. We've also discussed how different types of people interact – how certain types are ideally suited to work together, while others are doomed to misunderstandings. In this chapter we'll look at some tools and concepts that can be applied when trying to sort out, or prevent, problems rooted in Human Technology.

What we are really talking about in this chapter is *change*, and how to bring it about. We may want someone to change their habit of arriving five minutes late for work every day, or of interrupting in meetings. We may want a whole department to change their traditional working practices, to take on new roles and learn new skills. We may want to change our own position – to increase our responsibilities, get a pay rise or a more senior job title. Perhaps we realise that we are standoffish and difficult to get to know, but we want people to trust us more, or to confide their problems to us. Or we may feel that people don't take us or our ideas seriously, that we don't get the recognition or attention we deserve. What can we do? How can we bring about such changes, in individuals, in groups, in organisations and in ourselves?

105

People *can* change – people *must* change

From what we've said so far in this book you might get the idea that by the time we're adults, we're all firmly set within our personalities, and that if we aren't perfectly suited to the job we're in, or matched with the colleagues we deal with day to day – tough, there's nothing to be done about it. This is very far from the truth. Change is at the core of every part of our lives, every moment of our days. Even the most apparently contented and satisfied person amongst us will admit to some desire for change, in themselves, their circumstances, others around them, their environment, or the outside world. And that's only the desire for change that they'll admit to, to themselves and to others. Inside, as we saw in Chapter 2, there are all sorts of forces pulling in different directions, all saying, 'Be different – satisfy this desire, or that need; meet that aspiration!'

When I talk to clients about their backgrounds in order to identify their primary and secondary Human Technology components, I explain the three constants in life. That is:

1 we start
2 we finish
3 in between we change.

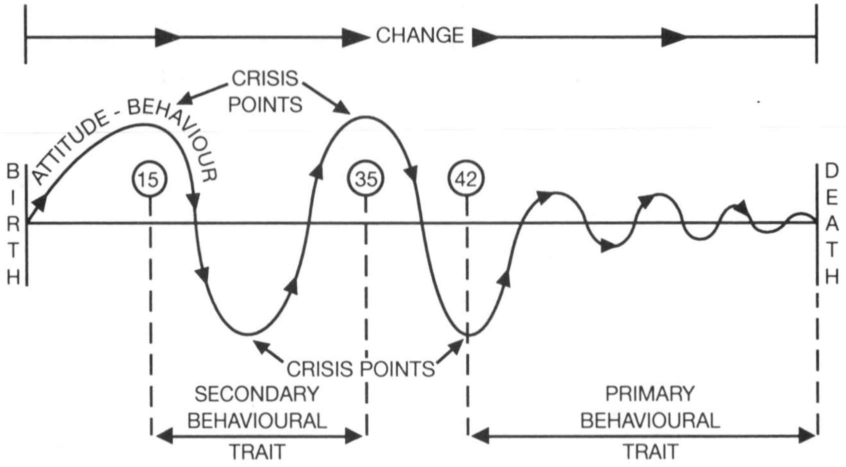

Fig. 6.1 Human Technology and the nature of change

The optimum path through life for each of us is where we manage our change with the least degree of struggle. Pain and struggle are a measure of an individual's resistance to change within themselves. Figure 6.1 illustrates that, fairly early in life we develop certain attitudes that are demonstrated in our behaviour, and these attitudes lead us in a certain direction. The straight, horizontal line (which is also a time-scale) represents the median – the easiest route through life – but it is an impossible target to achieve. As a result of our behaviour, we sometimes get off track – more so earlier in life, less so later on. So early on, possibly at school, we find ourselves way off track and feel that life isn't working. It could be a lack of study and the answer we perceive is to knuckle down and do some work – so we 'change', and our behaviour comes back towards the median.

The stage at which we decide to change, I label a 'crisis point' (usually because it's associated with a crisis in our lives). After we change, we usually overshoot and then reach another crisis point at the other extreme (so for students it could be studying too much and neglecting relaxation, hobbies, developing friendships and so on). This process of correction, over-correction, recorrection, etc carries on, but becomes less dramatic – it evens out closer to the median line as we get older, basically because we learn a little each time we perceive the need for change.

Superimposed over this time-scale in Figure 6.1 is, first, our *secondary*, and then (switching, roughly between ages 35 and 42) our *primary* Human Technology behaviour trait. In this latter stage we feel much more balanced: the fluctuations between corrections become less dramatic and we feel much more comfortable with ourselves.

A Performer-General at the transition

Eight years ago, I advised a client who was a Performer-General. This was quite unusual in itself, in that only 5 per cent or 6 per cent of my clients have both parts of their personality involving the different styles of leadership. What happens with these people is that they have to give instructions and direction, but because peace and quiet is very difficult for them – they have to emit energy (rather than receive it) all the time – they find listening almost an impossibility.

In the early years of his career, this guy was exploring his secondary 'General' component. But when I met him eight years ago (when he was aged 33) he was getting very dissatisfied with the structure and order in his life and was feeling very constrained. I explained to him that, between ages 35 and 42, he would switch from appreciating the value of order and structure to wanting to discard that aspect of his personality in favour of exploring his dominant Performer characteristics.

He called me out of the blue recently, three days after his 41st birthday. He explained that two months ago he'd left the company he'd been with for 20 years and set up his own business, and that he'd made more money in the past 2 months than in the previous 5 years. He's now 'flying' – exploring his fiery, entrepreneurial, solo, Performer personality.

107

Change can come about in a multitude of different ways. At the end of the day, however, true change has to be internal. It has to involve a recognition of the mismatch between conscious and unconscious, between self and surroundings, between aspirations and reality. The degree of ease with which we manage change in ourselves is the measure of the ease with which we get through life. The rhythm of change may vary, as may the rates of change, but change is constant in life nevertheless. It is part of the maturation process, part of growing up, part of education. The different Human Technology types handle change differently. Performers welcome change, and thrive on it. Their lives are fast-paced and constantly in motion. Nurses are receptive to change, while Generals fight change, but will accept it when logically convinced of its necessity. Soldiers are the slowest and most resistant to change.

People can be helped to change. In some cases, it can be a pleasant, rewarding task – helping the shy reserved character to reveal his or her opinions, to speak out and learn to participate. Sometimes it can be much more unpleasant – telling someone that their performance is not up to expectations, or that their colleagues find them difficult and abrasive. But actually in each case the stages of internal change are the same. And the consequences of ignoring the need for change are the same – namely friction and conflict.

STAGES OF CHANGE

There are four stages or levels in the process of change; spiritual, intellectual, emotional and physical.

1 **The spiritual level** At this level all we have is an idea, or maybe the germ of an idea, that change is a possibility. We may not have any conscious knowledge of a need or wish for change. For example, someone might ask you, 'Where do you live – what's your home like?' You might reply, 'Oh, I live in a lovely old house, done up just how I like, in a really nice area, convenient for work.' You've got no feeling of need or desire for change. But out of the blue one day comes a notion that it would be a good idea to move. You wonder, 'Where did that come from? The last thing I want to do is move. This house represents everything I have ever wanted, everything I've dreamed of !' That's the germ of an idea about change. It's the first indication that something within you is discontented and wants a change. It could be that somewhere inside you a little voice is saying, 'Is this really it? Does this house really represent everything I've ever wanted? Couldn't I achieve more? Have I set my sights too low?' or, 'All of my energy is spent making sure that I don't lose this house – every ounce of my creativity goes into work I don't find rewarding in itself, in order to pay the mortgage and upkeep on this place.' People who listen to their instincts – their inner voice – know themselves well enough to recognise this level of change, and are ready to consider what to do about it. Maybe they don't need to move, but to recognise the real reasons behind that flash thought 'It would be nice to move.'

2 **The intellectual level** When – as is very often the case – we do not pay attention to the germ or seed of an idea at the spiritual level, then the next stage, the intellectual level, comes into play. But there may well be a number of years between the spiritual and the intellectual stages. At the intellectual level, what happens is that the germ of the idea takes on a more realistic form. So we may discover that real events and circumstances take place that mean that the idea of moving home increases in attractiveness: for example, our favourite neighbours may move out and are replaced by people we don't like, or it's decided to build a motorway at the bottom of our garden. So we come to notice rational, intellectual signposts that lead us to the conclusion that this is not such a great place to live any more.

3 **The emotional level** If we don't pay any attention to the attractiveness of the idea of change, we then enter the emotional stage. This is where our level of comfortableness reduces and our level of uncomfortableness increases – we begin to feel uneasy or anxious. Suddenly the noise of the neighbour's children playing in their garden may seem unbearably irritating, the need to repaint the window sills yet again

seems like a huge pointless labour and expense. You don't get the same joy and satisfaction from the house that you used to. There's a certain unease about continuing to live in this house.

4 **The physical level** If we continue to pay no attention to the need for change, we enter the physical level and the 'unease' becomes 'disease'. Our bodies (which are wonderful barometers on what is going on in our lives) start to reflect the pain and struggle of our resistance to change. Pain is a measurement of our resisting our change – it could be an intellectual change, it could be a physical change, it could be any change. It could be the way we think about things. It could be small, it could be large, but we cannot 'not' change.

Action

Think back. Have you ever said to yourself (or anyone else), 'I'm in a rut'? What did you do about it? Did you dismiss the thought as silly and time-wasting? Did you think, 'Well, there's nothing I can do about it'? Did some well-meaning 'adviser' point out all the good things in your life, and suggest you count your blessings? Well, one way to think of a rut is as an open-ended grave. You're just continuing along, relying on possibly (or probably) outmoded habits or rules to help you make your decisions and set your agendas. Instead of allowing yourself to continue in the rut, you should think about ways to change your life – to satisfy the drive for change within you – and take the opportunity to do something about the early stages of the drive for change, without reaching the 'pain' stage.

109

HELPING CHANGE TO HAPPEN

So, what can you do to encourage beneficial change? To help others through the changes they need to make? To make the changes you want without losing things you value and want to retain? To cope with change – your own and other people's, particularly in the corporate context – you need to learn to communicate and, more fundamentally, to tell the truth.

Lies bind me; the truth sets me free.

This means learning to speak about what matters to you, to listen to others, to shape your message to a form that suits the receiver and to be constantly aware of the messages others are sending all the time. There is no set time or way to communicate – it happens constantly.

Indeed it's paradoxical that we spend such a large proportion of our lives talking to other people, but we seem to have enormous difficulties about telling each other the truth. It seems to me that in business, telling the truth to the people we work with is paramount in the organisation and running of an effective commercial operation.

Not telling the truth is not simply telling lies. We hint, we're subtle, we mislead, we infer, we assume, we imply, we expect, we keep our fingers crossed. Some people regard this as simply oiling the wheels of communication – that we cannot and should not be brutally frank with each other all the time. But people who are not open have to be closed: if you are not telling the truth for you, what actually are you saying, and how do people know what your position is?

If you feel it isn't safe to tell the truth, consider for a moment the amount of energy that goes into telling stories and avoiding telling the truth – it represents an enormous toll on the emotions and your brain processing resources (to avoid being found out you have to remember which stories you have told to which people). But once you decide you are just going to tell the truth you are saved all this effort and energy – telling the truth is effortless, euphoric, and easy. People know where you stand – they may not like it but they know what you stand for – and you go up in their estimation.

110

Communication – the key

Communication is the essential tool of human technology. No progress can be made without stating your objectives, your needs, listening to those of others, coming to mutual decisions, making sure that you all know the game plan.

WHAT IS COMMUNICATION?

You might think that simply stating what you want, plan or decide is easy, and that you already do it. But do you? Think about the following examples, in which Joan thinks she's communicated her intentions to the others in her team.

Intended communication:

'The board has decided to give the development of Project X to one particular team, and they've asked me to give them a report on everyone's individual workload and skills. That way they can decide whether our team is the best placed to take on the new project. This would be a really nice project for our team, and we'd all find it interesting and good for our careers, so we should try and get it.'

Example 1:

Joan: I'm compiling a report on the workload and skills of everyone in the team for the board – can you all let me know what jobs you've got on at the moment?

Reaction: Oh no! something's going on – they're planning to cut staff from this team. We'd better make our jobs list look as full and important as possible, so that the board feels they can't cut anyone from here.

Result: When Joan hands in the report, the board decides that her team is far too busy to take on this major project, and allocates it elsewhere.

Problem: Joan only communicated part of the story – leaving the team to make the wrong guesses as to what the missing bit was.

Example 2:

Joan: We might be the team to do the development on Project X – it'd be a great coup to get it!

Reaction: Team sits back and waits for board decision – they don't realise they're supposed to do anything.

Result: Board thinks Joan's team is too busy or too inefficient to do a report, so they don't give them the development project.

Problem: Again, Joan left out part of her communication – this time the action and strategy she'd decided on.

Example 3:

Joan (to Bill, another team member, in the coffee room): I'm putting together a report for the board on what we're up to as a team. I'll need details from everyone about what they're working on at the moment. If we can show that we can handle it, we might have a chance to take on the development of Project X – a great opportunity, don't you think?

Bill (thinks): Great – we'll be discussing that at the next group meeting – I won't talk to the others until then, in case I give them the wrong end of the stick, or leave anything out.

Result: At the next team meeting Joan expects all the others to be ready with their work breakdown summaries, and is furious that Bill hasn't told the others to get them ready.

Problem: Because Joan used an inappropriate context in which to make this communication (informal, only to one person) she hadn't succeeded in communicating her message, even though she actually said all of it.

The three examples above are all cases of poor communication even in situations uncomplicated by the additional factors of emotion, antagonism, or insecurity. If Joan had felt uncomfortable about taking on Project X, she might have communicated the information to her team, but slanted so as to make it seem an undesirable thing to take on. Then if their group report suggested to the board that her team was not suitable to do it, she could feel that the decision was nothing to do with her. If she was disliked by her team, because of an overbearing and autocratic manner, they might resent all her instructions, and react badly to any communications from her – perhaps 'hearing' only that they've got 'yet another form to fill in', and ignoring the message about the purpose and potential benefits of the report.

Assumptions

We tend to make assumptions about what other people already know in a given situation, or about their attitude to it. For instance, in the example above, if Joan starts from the assumption that her team already know what Project X is, and that there's a chance they could get to handle it, she won't start by introducing them to the project, explaining what it's about, talking about why it's a good thing for the team to work on and so on. Instead, she'll launch straight in to the report procedures and could well be annoyed by the lack of response and air of confusion with which her enthusiasm is greeted.

Joan may be keen to take on the new project, but if the team members are feeling already overloaded and stretched, the idea of taking on more may be depressing rather than exhilarating. If she realises this, she'll start her introduction to Project X with the idea that they may be going to unload some of their existing work in order to take on this new job. That way she's likely to get a positive response, not encounter the immediate barrier of, 'Oh no! *More* work!'. However, if she assumes that the others will be as enthusiastic as she is – the kind of attitude a Performer might be expected to display – she may feel disillusioned and disappointed when, instead of displaying the kind of forward-looking, positive approach she feels herself, the others seem to be more concerned with niggling worries and petty day-to-day concerns.

Hidden messages and loaded statements

'When I say X, I really mean Y, but I don't want to talk about Y directly. I'm sure you'll know I mean Y anyway.'

Sometimes we are reluctant to come straight out with what we mean.

We skirt around a subject, hoping that the other parties to the conversation will understand our message without our having stated it explicitly. Afterwards, we may look back on a conversation, and be convinced that we *did* communicate everything we wanted, and then be surprised and annoyed when action is taken only on what we said, not what we meant. For example:

Joan (to Bill, one of the team members): What about you and Jim working on planning the computer programming for Project X?

Bill: Well, I'm not sure if Jim would be the best person . . . (thinks: 'Oh no! Jim is terrible to plan things with – he's so disorganised, so sloppy. Sure, he understands the computers, but he's no good at teaching others, and I can never get him to proceed step by step, and note down what he's doing!')

Joan: Why not? Has he got a lot of other urgent work on? Or is there someone else who's better at programming?'

Bill: No, Jim's great at *programming*.

Joan: Are you worried that he doesn't understand the project?

Bill: I think *he* understands it, I'm worried about the others in the team.

Joan: Oh don't worry about them, I'll make sure everyone has really thorough briefings before we start.

113

Bill may think he's communicated his reservations to Joan – but without overtly criticising his colleague. Joan may be a bit puzzled by Bill's lack of enthusiasm for working with Jim, but certainly has no inkling of Bill's serious doubts about Jim's organisational and planning ability. This situation could easily develop into a major cause of friction. If when things get busy, Joan finds that the programming has been done in a haphazard manner, and that no one can understand Jim's instructions, she's going to allocate the blame to both Bill and Jim. Bill will feel resentful for taking the blame – his reasoning is that he warned Joan that Jim was sloppy and disorganised and expressed doubts from the start about his appropriateness for the role. Joan will be very annoyed by this attitude, as according to her memory, Bill never mentioned these doubts to her!

Often the hidden message we hope to convey without words is an emotional one – something we feel we can't openly admit to. Performers and Nurses are much better at expressing themselves about emotional and personal issues, while Generals and Soldiers feel that these sorts of things shouldn't be part of professional communication.

Misattributions

*'When you say **X** I know you mean **Y**.'*

Just as in speaking we may wish to communicate hidden messages, in listening we may think we hear hidden messages! These can be correct, in cases where we have managed to interpret someone else's 'between the lines' text properly. But all too often our interpretation is wildly out.

In most cases, our wrong interpretations result in a misattribution of the reasons why people do or say something. This can have a lot to do with our overall perception of that person, their role, or their status with respect to us. It also has a lot to do with our own self-perception. If we are insecure and vulnerable (a particular characteristic of Nurses), we might interpret even the most innocuous of comments as an insult or slight.

Example 1:

David: We don't need to order any more letterhead for ages – we've got enough to last for years!

Lorna's interpretation: He thinks I've been over-ordering, and he's checking up on me!

Behind David's message: Our use of normal letterhead is about to drop drastically, because all standard letters will be generated complete off the computer, rather than typed one by one.

Example 2:

Mark: This project has been exhausting and we've all put in lots of overtime. Why don't you take Friday off, Charles, and have a long weekend?

Charles' reaction: What's going on? He *never* cares if we're so tired we're asleep on our feet! There must be some reason he doesn't want me around on Friday.

Projection

In communication terms, projection means the situation in which you 'project' your ideas, opinions, and values on to the other people in the conversation or debate. So if you would react with disgust to a commercial suggestion that you thought of as fraudulent or dubious, you might assume that others would see it that way as well. It's very important to keep in mind however, that your personal system of learned values can never be identical to that of others – it's based on everything your parents and teachers taught you as a child, together with all your own experiences of dealing with the world. Even simple things like what you might find enjoyable can't be expected to transfer to others.

Anne: We're taking you out on Friday for your leaving do, Melanie – the whole office is going to a Karaoke evening at 'Fluffs' the singles bar. It'll be a real laugh – you'll have a great time!

Melanie's reaction: How can they possibly think I will enjoy that? I'm sure they'll expect me to sing, and that kind of public performance is just purgatory to me!

Forecasting

Often in communicating with others, we find ourselves building a lengthy 'scenario-in-the-air': 'If I tell him that, he'll be cross, and will say so-and-so. I won't put up with that so I'll have to really let him know what I think of him . . .' None of this imaginary conversation has actually taken place, but the picture you've created is so vivid that it's hard not to begin to experience the emotions involved in it. This is particularly true of stressful or confrontational conversations, and is a major factor in conflict.

115

Sometimes, even when a forecast communication has gone quite differently in reality from the expected scenario, it's impossible to rid your mind of the former, and your memory of the actual meeting becomes tinged with the version you expected. At worst, you may even believe (see the 'Misattributions' section above) that the other person really *meant* to communicate all the things you'd forecast in advance, and you therefore dismiss what was actually said as a deliberate attempt to deceive you!

Yes, this does sound a bit like paranoid behaviour. But we can all be insecure about ourselves, our roles, our responsibilities and our performance. If we don't much like and respect ourselves, it's easy to assume that others feel the same way, and to believe that pleasant supportive communications are merely a polite mask for real feelings.

Starting from common ground

Any communication, particularly that taking place in conflict or friction situations, must start from a common basis. All parties involved need to know what the topic is, the background, the targets and the time pressures. An essential element of defining the common ground is to set and answer the question: 'What are we trying to achieve here?'

Always remember what kind of people you are dealing with in your communications. When you're communicating to a Performer, you have to remember that he has the attention span of a gnat. If you can't say what you want to say in two or three minutes then don't bother to start. So you really need to be clear about what you want to communicate to a Performer, to plan the content and condense it to bullet points if necessary. Because they are right-brained, Performers rebel against preamble, analysis, reasoning, etc – they just want to know what action is required.

Generals on the other hand are very good listeners – they like meetings and discussions and can sit for long periods, analysing and summarising what is being said, picking out the important things and discarding the unimportant things. So communicating with Generals is much easier – they tend to enjoy it because they are good at it.

Soldiers will also be able to sit for long periods listening, but they may well be slow to grasp the gist of what is being communicated to them. Repetition may well be necessary, supported by diagrams or pictures or a demonstration showing them what it is you want them to do. Once they have grasped the points then they will be able to carry out the role or task for ever afterwards.

All Nurses want to know when you are communicating with them is do you like them? Being liked and nurtured in a relationship is the most important thing for them, so authority figures communicating with Nurses must make it clear that they are liked and cared about. If they feel this affection is missing it can hurt and throw them off balance for considerable periods – hours, and sometimes days – so it's very damaging and expensive if authority figures do not develop the skills needed in talking to Nurses. This means that it must be more than an impersonal, dry relationship – there must be an emotional content ('How was your weekend?'; 'You look nice today'; and so on). As soon as a Nurse is convinced you like and care about her then she will work very hard for you.

Good communication practices

Have a look at these two conversations, between marketing director Fraser, and Trevor, the senior sales person, who is a Performer, and renowned for his cavalier attitude to sales meetings. By rights, Trevor should actually organise sales meetings, plan the agenda and act as chair, as well as giving the opening presentation. In fact, he rarely remembers what day the meeting's been set for, or who's coming, and, even if he remembers to attend, seldom has a presentation prepared, or any figures compiled. Fraser knows this, and has therefore taken on the task of planning sales meetings himself. In the first conversation, Fraser makes plain his resentment of Trevor's 'unprofessional' disorganisation . . .

Fraser: Since *I've* got to sort out the sales meeting I need to know what you're going to talk about, and when. You haven't told me yet what your presentation is going to be about, or where you want it placed on the agenda, or how long you're going to speak. How am I supposed to get it all sorted out if you don't tell me what you're planning?

Trevor: Oh, don't worry about it – it'll be fine! There's plenty of time.

Fraser: No there isn't – It's next week! Do you even know what day it's going to be on?

Trevor: Friday, I suppose, as usual?

Fraser: There you are – no, it's not on Friday, as you ought to know! At the last meeting it was decided to hold them mid-week in future, as so many people had already booked Fridays off!

Trevor: Well, what day *is* it on?

Fraser: Wednesday!

Trevor: Well, that's fine – you just tell me when you want me to be there, and what you want me to talk about, and I'll do the usual.

Fraser: That's no good – this is supposed to be *your* responsibility. I don't know what's been happening in Sales – you do. You ought to be giving them a report on recent sales figures, and talking about new developments.

117

Trevor: Oh, don't fuss, I'll do a report.

What do you think? It seems unlikely that Trevor will turn up on time to the meeting, prepared to talk about relevant matters, and carrying a report for the other sales people. But if Fraser had tried to encourage and support rather than bully him, things might have been different . . .

Fraser: What are you planning for the sales conference next week?

Trevor: Oh, next week is it? I'd forgotten. What day is it?

Fraser: Wednesday – starting at 10.00. Are you making a formal presentation that you'd like me to put on the agenda?

Trevor: I hadn't really thought about it – I'm not sure what to talk about . . .

Fraser: Didn't you tell me you'd had some interesting customer feedback on the new product range – what about speaking about that? It would be useful for the others.

Trevor: Oh yes – I suppose that would be a good idea. And maybe I could give a run-down on how I got on on my last European trip.

Fraser: Yes, that's a great idea. I think it would help inspire the others if you could tell them about your successes. I'm sure there are valuable lessons to be learned – especially if there's any figures you could show them.

Trevor: OK, I could get some figures together.

Fraser: Tell you what, would you like to go through the figures with Sarah? She could write them up into a handout, which could be passed out before your talk.

Trevor: Right, thanks – I don't know when I'd have had time to do a report, but if I can brief Sarah and she sorts it all out, that'd be fine.

Fraser: That's great. How about if you speak last thing in the morning, before lunch, at 12.00, for about half-an hour? Then at lunch you could sit with the area sales heads and give them a chance to ask questions.

Trevor: Sounds fine to me!

Fraser: Good, I'll get Sarah to come in to your office this afternoon to start work.

Fraser may well be thinking, 'Trevor's never going to get this ready on his own', but he hasn't said it. Instead he's made sure that Trevor has been informed about and become interested in the meeting, and that by giving him an assistant whom he's ready to accept, and a target he's ready to meet, and a chance to shine (very important for Performers), he's done everything he can to get Trevor prepared.

118

There are a few good practices to keep in mind in communication – trying not to let your irritation drive the tone of the communication (as in the first example above) is one of them! Others include:

- organisation: present ideas clearly in an orderly fashion
- brevity when speaking: don't go on and on – it's boring
- give-and-take: let others have their say; most communication should be in the form of a dialogue, not a lecture
- establish a common vocabulary
- avoid 'loaded' language
- learn to listen
- take responsibility for checking that your message has been understood, and that you've understood the messages you've received
- ask for feedback – and provide it yourself.

Some of these points are self-evident – brevity and organisation, for example. If you've got a limited list of points to make, *make* them, don't let them get lost in a mass of information and detail. If they are controversial, and will need discussion, try and give a brief, complete outline first, and then go through each point one by one, allowing others to have their say.

Common vocabulary

Establishing a common vocabulary can be harder than you think. Misunderstandings are so frequent that they can be hard to pin down and correct. Is 'the next meeting' the one later today, or the one in a month's time? When you tell someone they are in a 'responsible' position, do you mean they are responsible for their own workload, reporting, data collection, etc, or that they are responsible for checking and directing the work of others? There are all sorts of cultural, regional, gender and educational influences on our use of language, and it's easy to use words that mean one thing to you, and quite another to their hearers. Be receptive to people's reactions to your message. If you get the feeling they are reacting negatively to something you thought carried a positive or neutral message, check that what you intended to convey was what got through. Try and clear up misunderstandings before they become embedded in memories.

Loaded language
Another sort of confusion over vocabulary is the use of 'loaded' words. To one person, calling someone an 'understanding' manager can suggest that they are soft and yielding, the kind of person who avoids confrontation and backs down in the face of aggression. To others it may mean willing to listen to others' points of view, flexible in their approach to staff, good with people.

119

Listening
Listening is a crucial communication skill. Careful listening ensures that *you've* got the right end of the stick, and avoids missing the main point. It can also help you to decide how well your message has got across. If the response to your suggestions seems defensive, was your message taken as aggressive?

Paraphrasing
Paraphrasing is useful for checking that you've understood correctly, and that others have understood you. Basically it means repeating back a message as you understand it. For example:

Sarah: I'd like to get agreement on that at the next meeting.

Janet: You'll put it on the agenda for the meeting this afternoon?

Sarah: Oh no, sorry. I meant the meeting in two weeks' time.

Sarah and Janet are both now clear when the item is to be discussed, but if Janet hadn't paraphrased Sarah's message back to her, she would have expected to deal with it that same day. It doesn't work if you simply repeat back the exact words of the speaker – they still have no idea that there is any confusion about their message.

Sarah: I'd like to get agreement on that at the next meeting.

Janet: You'll put it on the agenda for the next meeting?

Sarah: Yes, I will.

Chalkcheese Ltd – the General and the Performer

Having got Natalie to withdraw her resignation, and Stuart to agree to her plan of campaign, Gail's next move is to try and bring Patrick into the plan, and to prevent him throwing any more spanners in the works! She's rather nervous about this, as she finds him very hard to predict, and therefore very hard to deal with.

Gail: Patrick – I'm glad I caught you! I just wanted to let you know we've cancelled the next think-tank meeting (which I'm sure you'll be glad of!) We've rescheduled for the following week at the same time. Will that be OK with you?

Patrick: Why has the meeting been cancelled? I didn't know about this?

Gail: Oh, we didn't want to bother you about it. We're going ahead with the data collection from the other departments, and I don't think there's any point in meeting until the responses are in. I've spoken to the computer man, Cliff Thompson, and he won't expect a further briefing until then.

Patrick: Now wait a minute! What's all this 'we'? And why are you communicating with Cliff without speaking to me – he's my contact. Are you trying to get me off the team?

Gail: No, no, you don't understand . . .

Patrick: Oh yes I do – you think that with me not around you can push Stuart and Natalie into doing whatever you want, so that you'll come out covered with glory. Well, I'm not putting up with it!

Gail realises that she has made the wrong approach to Patrick. Because she thinks that he doesn't enjoy meetings and paperwork, she thought he'd be glad to avoid them. But he knows that meetings and paperwork are the stepping stones to rewards and status in business – which he wants. The shouting match at the last meeting left Patrick feeling very confused – he's been doing his best for the think-tank and no one seems to appreciate it. Now they are all working around him, and leaving him out. He feels stepped over, and hurt.

Feedback

Feedback is crucial in communication – identify what has pleased, annoyed, hurt, or confused you, and tell the truth to the person who has caused these reactions. If you do not, communication is not happening. Sometimes you'll find that annoying or confusing messages are a result of one of the forms of miscommunication discussed above. Only by using feedback can any misunderstandings be cleared up.

120

Feedback in conflict situations should be selective, effective, and care should be taken to avoid exaggeration. When trying to defend a position you feel strongly about, it's easy (in the interests of the argument) to overstate your case and to forget or minimise points of compromise. Feedback should never take the form of a personal attack.

> **Discussion is an exchange of knowledge; argument is an exchange of ignorance.**

Have a look at the following examples. At the last department meeting, Angela presented a new timetable for staff to take it in turns to cover the evening shift – always unpopular. A recent resignation means that everyone has to take on some extra duty as a matter of urgency. Angela is a General, so is very thorough and organised, but perhaps a little careless about the feelings of the people she's dealing with. Rather than consulting with everyone, she's sorted out a new rota, and simply announced it. No one was very pleased, but Frank was particularly upset. Under the old rota he never covered Tuesday evenings, and had arranged an evening class for that day. Under the new rota he would have to miss three classes before the end of term.

121

Some inappropriate feedback . . .

■ Frank says nothing in the meeting, but complains to the others over coffee and during breaks. Some of the other staff thought the new rota announcement was a bit high-handed, but as none of them have been directly disrupted in the way Frank has, they didn't bother to say anything. but they all agree that 'It's not fair' and 'She'd no right' and so on. So when Frank next encounters Angela in the corridor, he says, aggressively, 'I've been talking to the others about the new rota. We all think it's really unfair! You should have consulted with us before drawing it up, and not just gone ahead on your own.'

This is inappropriate for lots of reasons – *poor choice of venue* (in an open corridor), *timing* (it would have been better to bring this up immediately in the meeting), *emotionally charged* (Frank's anger is bound to make Angela defensive), *and it's not actually true*. Frank's real concern is for his missed evening class, but he's unwilling to look as if he's only worried about himself, so he's set himself up as the representative of the rest of the staff. This is going to make Angela feel very isolated, and make her react badly to the rest of the group.

■ Frank asks to speak to Angela in her office after the meeting. He begins: 'About the new rota. I'd really rather not do Tuesday evenings. I've got a class that night and I don't want to miss it.' Angela is annoyed, 'It's a bit late to tell me that now – why didn't you say something before?' Frank replies, 'I didn't know you were revising the rota until you came to the meeting with it all finalised. I didn't get a chance to discuss it with you!' Angela is still irritated, 'You should have brought it up in the meeting – everyone's got the new rota now. But I suppose we'll have to look at it again.' Frank feels really aggrieved, and is hardly listening to her. 'You're always imposing things on us without discussion! You don't pay any attention to our views at all!'

Although Frank has now chosen a better venue for this conversation, his timing is still poor. Angela has given out the rota, and everyone expects to follow it. He's also not listening properly. She has agreed to redo the rota. Finally, he's exaggerating and confusing the issue by making a broad accusation of Angela's overly authoritarian attitude. All of this is counter-productive, and even if Frank gets the rota amended the way he wants, his relationship with Angela is going to be damaged.

More appropriate feedback . . .

■ During the meeting, after Angela has presented the rota, Frank speaks up: 'I realise that it's essential to get a new rota set up, and that we must rearrange coverage quickly. I know we'll all have to take on some extra evenings, and I'm sure everyone else does. I do have a problem with the evenings specifically allocated to me – they conflict with a commitment I have already arranged. A different day of the week would be much better for me. This may be the case for others as well. Could we all give our day preferences now, and try and sort out a rota that we're all happy with, but which makes sure we have complete evening coverage at the same time?'

This has stated Frank's personal objections, and opened the floor to allow others to come forward with theirs. But it has also recognised why Angela has tried to go ahead and get the problem sorted out quickly. If Angela is the kind of authoritarian General who finds it difficult to take criticism, she may still react badly to this 'mutiny', but at least things have begun on an amicable and non-emotional level. Also, everyone is involved, and things are open. If Angela is a good General, she'll quickly realise that this is *not* a challenge to her authority, and not something to get wound up about, and instead will concentrate on getting a workable solution that everyone feels a part of and happy with. In arriving at solutions, good Generals deal only with the facts of a matter, not the emotions.

Venue

Choosing the right venue for important communications can make all the difference to how well your message gets across. In the first example above, Frank made the mistake of speaking to Angela in the corridor. Her mind will almost certainly have been on other things, and their conversation is very likely to be overheard or interrupted.

Some communications are best conducted in a formal way – a time and place for a meeting should be set, the parties should arrange not to be disturbed, and possibly an agenda for the meeting should be agreed in advance. Other types of communication are better done 'on-the-spot', with no lead in. For example, if you need to administer a minor reprimand to a staff member – for lateness, sloppy work, inappropriate behaviour to customers or spending too long on personal phone calls or chat – it may be best to seize the moment when the person is 'red-handed' to speak to them.

Ideally you should never reprimand someone in front of others, as this is very demeaning. However, calling her aside and saying, 'I think you were a bit sharp with that customer – I know he was being very difficult, but you must keep your temper and not argue back. Try and distance yourself, and not take things too personally.' This approach should mean that she relates the reprimand to the undesirable behaviour, but that she doesn't feel diminished by it. If she starts to argue with you, suggest that you then move venues and discuss it privately. If you have to give the same reprimand again, then set up a formal occasion on which to talk about it.

123

The venue for any sort of conflict communication can have a major effect on the power base of the conflict. If two people of equal status have to discuss an issue on which they differ, agreeing to meet in one or other's office or 'home territory' conveys an immediate advantage to the one 'at home'. Such meetings should always be held in a 'neutral' venue. On the other hand, if one person is in a more powerful position than the other, taking the discussion into the 'weaker' person's territory gives them a boost, and may help them to come forward with their opinions and arguments more freely.

The best communication requires a 'to-and-fro' approach. There's no point in continuing down a preplanned path if, as soon as you start, you get some knowledge that you didn't have before. Be prepared to stop, and listen, to receive feedback, and to modify or even drop your plan or argument. But at the same time, make sure your contribution is not swamped by the interruption. If you have other things to say which are still relevant, don't go silent, or allow yourself to be shouted down.

Action

Admitting a mistake or lack of information can be a powerful tool for defusing potential conflict situations. It's very hard to work up, or keep up, a feeling of resentment against an opponent in an argument who says, 'Sorry, I didn't know that', or, 'I shouldn't have done that.' Always be prepared to admit a fault – it is not a sign of weakness, it is a sign of strength.

Action

When communicating in a meeting or group situation:

- *don't wait for someone else to speak for you or your ideas*

- *don't hog the floor*

- *don't meander*

- *don't get bogged down.*

Keeping tempers even

This book is all about conflict – avoiding it, curing it and cleaning up afterwards. In conflict situations, keeping one's temper is one of the hardest things to do, yet one of the most important. As well as keeping yourself calm, avoid aggravating others – the aim should always be to resolve differences, not inflame them.

124

Some suggestions:

- separate the personal issues from the professional;
- identify your own feelings about the topic before you speak;
- don't allow bias to colour your statements;
- don't wave red rags at bulls!

Some of these thoughts may imply that there are ideas that shouldn't be brought into conflict discussions. Not so. It *is* important to bring up even difficult personal feelings, and to discuss and resolve them. The key idea – always – is tell the truth.

Performers – very instinctive people – tend to feel attacked when their ideas are scrutinised in an aggressive way. It's a bit like challenging an artist about the 'validity' of his latest painting. When an idea is challenged, there can often be very little defence for it (unless a detailed study has taken place of costs, ramifications, etc). Performers are no good at this detailed assessment – the main thing they are good at is coming up with ideas. Usually, nine out of ten of these ideas are rubbish, but the tenth could well be a gem.

Nurses rarely propose ideas, but, if they did, would certainly feel very discouraged and swamped if their instinctive idea was challenged, ridiculed or rejected.

Soldiers and Generals are more thick-skinned. Attacks on them will be unsuccessful – they are more likely to attribute the emotion to weakness and instability in the attacker than to something he or she feels is highly important and to which they are deeply committed.

Decision making and compromise

Communication in a conflict situation is all about resolving the conflict. At some point, the conflict has to stop, or business becomes impossible. A key thing to remember is that there doesn't have to be a winner and a loser in every conflict situation. It may seem like a difficult concept, but the end-result to aim for is a win-win situation. This is the situation where all parties feel that they can live with the solution; that they haven't had to give up important points of principle; or that they are left without their point of view having been satisfactorily explored.

Sure, in a conflict of direct opposites, there may have to be a negotiated compromise, a half-way house. But care should be taken to view this, and present it to the outside world, as a new option, not as a result which offends the least number of people even while it pleases none.

125

Not all conflicts contain a problem that needs to be resolved. Conflicts may be about apparent problems, which vanish when communication is established, when people tell the truth about their positions and feelings, and take the time to listen to those of others. Or the conflict may be entirely separate from, and obscuring, the problem. We'll look further at the different ways in which conflicts, problems and compromises can be related and handled in later chapters.

The recap

If an agreement is reached that involves a practical strategy, everybody concerned must be absolutely clear what it is. A good idea is to have a 'cooling-off' period between reaching an agreement and then 'recapping' it. That way, if people feel after a meeting or series of meetings that they still haven't sufficiently covered an important point, or that they didn't do their argument justice, they have time to gather their thoughts. A written version of what's been agreed is useful, as is checking that everyone's understanding of the agreement is the same. Finally, the practical implications of any decision must be made crystal clear: what's to be done next; who by; time scale; budgets; level of publicity/secrecy and so forth.

COMMUNICATION CHANNELS

Your business or organisation may already have systems of meeting, reporting, assessment and discussion in place. However, it is worth thinking about these formal communication channels and considering what roles they fill, how they overlap and if there are any omissions. If all meetings consist of formal reports from junior levels to more senior levels, then these are unlikely to be sources of creative ideas and problem solving in themselves.

Other sorts of meeting, which may be more productive and innovative are, for example, the quality-circle model or the work-team model.

Quality circles

Each quality circle consists of a small number of employees (4 to 15), who all do similar work, and report to the same manager. There may be many quality circles in a large operation. Each circle meets regularly, with the goal of identifying and analysing problems its own members encounter at work, and providing solutions. Membership of a quality circle is voluntary – employees are encouraged to join, not told to.

One of the benefits employees experience personally is an increased feeling of control over their job environment, pace and order. Members of a circle receive training, both from each other and from outside experts, in the technical aspects of their job, and in skills such as problem solving and making presentations to management. New members of staff have an opportunity to get the benefit of the years of experience of others, without interrupting the work process, while people with more up-to-date training can pass on new ideas. Teaching people how to communicate and to present their ideas clearly to colleagues and supervisors is one way to remove potential sources of friction due to hierarchical divisions at work.

The quality circle involves all employees, at all levels, in the setting of long- and short-term objectives. This participatory approach makes it easier to remove any obstacles preventing the achievement of agreed objectives. Other benefits of quality circles include improved commitment to necessary changes in work practices. Involving people at all levels in decision making, in investigating new developments and comparing systems means that everyone feels more empowered and in control if the decision is taken to alter working practices. No one can claim that the decision is a 'bolt from the blue', or feel destabilised by it.

The quality circle is an integral part of the management system in Japan, and the key to its success there appears to be the involvement of all grades of staff. Quality circles, working properly, have been shown to improve productivity, product quality and safety at work, as well as reducing waste, improving communication between management and workers, creating a problem-solving environment, increasing job involvement, and improving morale.

We talked earlier about the problems of setting up successful quality circles in a country of Generals (like England) rather than a country of Soldiers (like Japan). Generals are personally ambitious, and less likely to be willing to put their best ideas into a common pool – for the common, rather than the personal, good. An alternative set-up could be the work team.

Work teams

Unlike quality circles, which tend to consist of people doing the same types of work, teams may consist of people doing very different sorts of work, drawn from different departments, but working on common projects. People may be members of several different teams. So, for example, in a book publishing company a team might consist of the editor responsible for contracting new projects on a particular topic, the marketing assistant responsible for promoting that list, the desk editor responsible for working on the text and content of those titles, the production controller who has to cost, progress and physically produce those titles, and the sales representative who has to sell the books into shops. Each team member may have roles in other teams – the sales representative, for instance, probably sells several other lists – and from time to time other people may become involved in the team, such as an additional desk editor when work is particularly heavy.

127

Members of the team work in their own departments but meet regularly to provide feedback on projects currently under way, new work expected, changes in the requirements from the rest of the company, and so on.

The value of a team is that each person in that team feels a commitment to the product or service they are producing. They have a sense of achievement when 'their' project is successful. It's useful for team members to practise talking to each other in a problem-solving scenario, so they learn that it is safe to contribute. Everyone in the team gains a clear understanding and overview of how the whole project works. Improvements in quality come about both through an increased pride in the 'stuff' of work and through better communication between all the different elements of the organisation.

INFLUENCING REACTIONS IN OTHERS – A CHECKLIST

- Change is a constant element in life – we all need to change, to recognise this need for change in both ourselves and others, and to cope with change.

- Communication and telling the truth are key elements in coping with change.

- Improving your communication skills means learning to:
  - organise your thoughts before speaking
  - listen
  - practise give-and-take
  - use paraphrasing
  - use feedback.

- Avoid miscommunications such as:
  - hidden messages
  - misattributions
  - projections
  - forecasting.

- Tailor your communications to be appropriate both to the message itself and to the receiver. A different approach is needed depending on whether you are communicating with a General, a Nurse, a Performer or a Soldier.

- Think about appropriate times and places for communications.

- Set up opportunities for creative communications among workmates.

7

Handling power games and authority

Chalkcheese Ltd – the battleground

Although Patrick is still angry about what he sees as Gail's 'manoeuvres', there has been progress. The questionnaires have come in from all the different departments, and Gail, Stuart and Natalie have painstakingly compiled the data from them. They've presented their findings to computer expert, Cliff Thompson, who has come to the think-tank to present his recommendations.

Cliff: . . . so, to summarise, both of these systems I recommend will do everything your departments are currently doing on their various different computers, and both will improve inter-departmental communications, information and data transfer, and boost planning and forecasting capacity.

Given the number of machines you need, system A is significantly cheaper and has the advantage of being readily available from several suppliers. There's also local service/maintenance facilities. System B is much more sophisticated, and initially I imagine you wouldn't begin to use all its features, let alone some of the new things currently being developed. It's going to be more expensive, and you won't be able to get many competitive quotes as there are only two or three suppliers.

But there's no doubt in my mind that Chalkcheese will benefit the more use its people can make of electronic information. System A could well be too limited for you in five years' time, and then you'd have to scrap it completely and start again. System B would be much easier to update and extend – it would make much better economic sense at that time.

Gail: Thank you very much Cliff, that was very clear and helpful. We'll need to study the details carefully, and we may have to come back to you with any queries, so that we can be really clear in our minds what we're going to recommend to the board.

Stuart: I think it's pretty obvious. System A does everything we asked, and is very much cheaper. I can't see the board wanting to throw cash at something we 'won't even use all of at present'!

Patrick: Now, wait a minute – we're trying to set this up for the future, not just for today. I can see lots of uses for system B, in marketing particularly. The extra facilities will allow us to do all sorts of new things.

Stuart: Like what?

Patrick: Well, I'm no computer boffin, but there's people in marketing who *are*, and they've said that it'll be a wonderful tool, allowing them to do really fine-tuned targeted stuff . . .

Natalie: It sounds a bit vague, Patrick. After all, we're already going to be proposing a much more sophisticated – and expensive – system than the board originally thought of. If we go to them with something we can't justify 100 per cent, then we risk them turning the whole thing down.

Stuart: I think we should just get Cliff to write up the full details on system A, and present only that to the board. We can present some competitive quotes, as well as an implementation plan. That'll be enough for them to get their heads around.

Patrick: You're just ignoring my opinion on this whole thing! System B is clearly the best option.

130

Conflicts in organisations are frequently caused by situations in which a power game is being played out – two parties on an equal level vying for their view to predominate. Indeed, the ways in which we can exercise power over others and establish a power base underlies all human relationships. This chapter shows what to do if you are in the middle, or on the edge of a power game; how to combat such situations and how to play them to your advantage.

What is power?

> **'Unlimited power is apt to corrupt the minds of those who possess it.'**
> William Pitt, Speech to the House of Lords, 9 January 1770

Power has been seen as both desirable and dangerous – as a concept which carries corruption with it, but at the same time, as something we must all strive for.

We start to learn about power as children – parents have power, children none. We learn that power is control, is the ability to impose our rules and preferences on others, and can result in sucking somebody else dry. If I can get you to do what I want, I feel nurtured and fed, you feel drained.

If you give some of your power to someone else, perhaps because you love them or trust them, or give them your loyalty in exchange for their love or loyalty, then if they turn away to do their own thing, even briefly, you feel they are not there for you, they have drained your power, diminished you, made you vulnerable.

You can think of power struggles as being like a see-saw (see Figure 7.1). If I feel down, I feel as if I'm on the 'down' end of the see-saw, and you, in comparison are 'up'. This may not be true; you have your own insecurities and you may not perceive yourself as 'above' me – but my perception is that you are up while I am down. My reaction therefore is to try and get you down, in the belief that your fall will result in my rise. It somehow seems hard to believe that we can both be up at the same time.

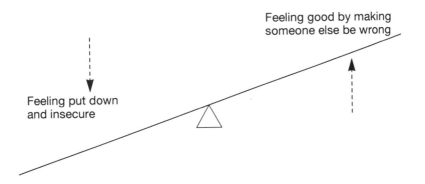

Fig. 7.1(a) The 'win/lose' see-saw in a power struggle
In a power struggle it is felt a good idea (either consciously or unconsciously) to put somebody else down, to put them in the wrong or to make them look foolish. If you succeed, your side of the see-saw goes up at the expense of the other side (person) which is lowered, indicating they feel put down.

Fig. 7.1(b) The 'win/win' see-saw
Here there is even keel maintained by avoiding pushing the other person down. When one side is down, feels vulnerable, lost and in need of help, the other restores equilibrium by talking, comforting and helping solve problems. They provide a supportive (what I would call an interdependent) relationship, which is two independent people sharing and leaning on each other. The relationship is 'on the level' and there is no put down. Instead there is:

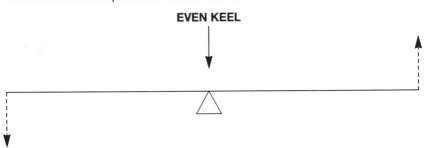

This attitude can result in constant little 'games' to score power points. For example, if we're working together and I say 'I'd love a coffee – could you make two coffees for us?' I'm asking you to do something for me, giving me power. I might not want coffee, you might not want coffee, but you're in the position where you can't really refuse without being rude, which would also give me points.

Power can exist for one person over another: formal organisational power, power of personality, etc. One sort of struggle is the attempt to reduce the other's power, to get some of one's own. Another sort of struggle is that between two people of equal power, trying to gain ascendancy over each other.

If you're my boss, and your job is to define my job, and help me perform it to defined standards, then once you've done that properly, you could almost say you have no 'power' over me (unless I give you some by failing to do my job properly). If I perform as you've instructed, then we are equal in terms of power. Many people fail to do the job of instruction properly, perhaps in order to leave things vague, to retain the power base they have by virtue of their position. If the goalposts are moved occasionally, keeping subordinates on their toes, then they can never achieve full power. This ploy is used often by insecure managers.

The subordinate has the power of being able to constantly challenge the senior to give better instruction, define the criteria. So, if the boss says 'You haven't done X properly, that's not good enough.', the subordinate can regain power, can wrong-foot him, by saying, 'I don't understand what I've done wrong. How do you want this done? What are your criteria?' This re-establishes his power base, putting the senior in the wrong for making unreasonable demands, failing to perform his instructional role properly. A subordinate who is trying to unseat a senior has many opportunities to increase his power level. You might think that all the power lies with the senior, but this is really not so. He may have the ability to threaten demotion, lack of promotion, loss of rewards (salary, bonus, benefits), or even sacking; but at the end of the day, his performance is being judged on the sum of the ability and performance of those under him, and a constant failure of his staff to achieve what they should will reflect badly on him.

What's the difference between power and authority?

The *Oxford English Dictionary* defines **authority** as 'power or right to enforce obedience; delegated power'; while **power** is defined as 'personal, political or social ascendancy'. This uneasy relationship of transferred power, power that is given by right of position rather than personal power, is at the root of many conflict situations in the workplace.

> **Surrender involves giving up control – but not losing power.**

Threats to authority can come from all sides. A subordinate member of staff can destabilise a manager in the ways described earlier. Colleagues and staff can bypass a manager who has nominal authority, but no real power. Seniors can undermine a manager's authority by refusing to back up her decisions, redeploying staff, giving her insufficient resources, or leaving her out of the chain of communication.

Generals in the Human Technology system relish authority. They want the recognition, the job title, but most of all they like taking responsibility for planning, for organising, and for instructing other people. Performers may confuse authority with status. They want status, want to be recognised for their own abilities and successes, but don't really enjoy having to take decisions for others, taking responsibility for others, or having others look to them for leadership. Neither Nurses or Soldiers are generally successful in positions of broad authority. However, within a circumscribed area, and under the right sort of conditions, they can both make good managers. In the case of Nurses, it's important that they must not be under too much pressure. Stress, difficult colleagues, staff or senior management, will all cause them to withdraw, and will provoke emotional rather than logical reactions to problems. Soldiers (given a specific course of action and a time-frame for delivery) can be excellent at implementing a plan, but will react badly to change, and will be slow to see the need for flexibility.

133

Power struggles – the leaders

The Human Technology types, therefore, most likely to be the cause of power struggles are the two 'leader' types – ie, people who are predominantly either Generals or Performers. Both want control. If a leader sees another leader as challenging his control, or in the way of his acquiring greater control, then a power struggle is the likely result. Even in an apparently amicable situation, there may be constant subtle power struggles under way which can destabilise the rest of the company.

Generals versus Generals

Generals battling against Generals are likely to do so in a planned, strategic manner. The conflict is likely to be a very covert and political affair, involving different interpretations of the rules and regulations.

Boardroom blazeups, sudden changes of policy and 'calls to arms' are not likely with Generals. As a result, the power struggle can be very difficult to pin down and identify. It may start with divisions between departments, subtly manipulated by the Generals who run them. Little niggles like:

'**They** never bother to let us know what they're doing.'

'You'll have to put that in writing, or **they'll** never admit to knowing about it.'

'He won't do that without an instruction from **them**.'

can reflect an underlying deep divide orchestrated by individuals trying to increase or hold on to their power base.

Someone confident in their role, secure in their authority, would soon stop this sort of thing, reminding staff that everyone in the organisation is working to the same end goal, and that although each group or department's own targets may differ from those of others, they all need to support and sustain each other. Such a manager would also call in other department managers and bring this sort of 'cold war' out into the open, saying:

'Look, there seems to be some problem between our departments. I keep hearing complaints from members of one department about members of the other, or accusations of poor performance, blame for errors, suggestions of incompetence and so on. What's going on? What can we do to stop this wasteful bickering?'

This is the kind of good communication that's needed to defuse potential conflict situations. The manager should specify examples of exactly what he's talking about, so that his opposite number has a chance to react to them. If the other department manager is not involved in a power struggle, this should immediately become clear. She should be willing to try and identify the source of the problem – it could be that each department is unclear about it's own role and goals, and the relationship between themselves and the other department. There could be some resentment because of an apparent inequality in status, rewards or conditions.

If there is a power struggle going on, opening up the channels of communication, forcing the other person to reveal more of what they are thinking and planning, can have the effect of adding fuel to the fire, but is much more likely to blow it out. Many times, the drive to gain more power is a result of a *feeling* of powerlessness, or vulnerability, rather than a realistic view of the actual situation. Once the real issues are being openly discussed, the real sources of power become much clearer.

After all, if you are taken seriously enough to discuss power struggles with, you must have some power yourself !

GENERALS VERSUS PERFORMERS – HOW THE CONFLICTS BEGIN

An international brokerage house with a problem

The firm was run by four partners. One was predominantly a Performer, while the other three were predominantly Generals, and they felt that the Performer was out of control, and that they couldn't cope with him. They found his behaviour too erratic and difficult to deal with. He was forever setting up new deals without consulting his partners – some of the deals were great, but others committed the firm to major transactions that often over-stretched its resources. So they asked their accountants for advice about controlling the situation. The accountants said 'This is not an accounting or a legal problem, it's a people problem', and suggested that the firm should call me in. I went to see them.

I talked about behaviourial skills and models to the Performer, who under-stood, but what he needed (and he actually volunteered this himself), was for his partners to be more authoritative. This is because the way to deal with Per-formers is similar to one's approach with small children. In essence, you say, 'Be quiet and listen to what I have to say.' They say, 'Great.' and have no problem with that.

135

I then discussed this approach with the other three partners and confirmed quite quickly that, as conservative and organised Generals, they were frightened of him: 'Oh my God, his behaviour is too difficult. He's like a firework that could go off at any moment. I go into my office, close the door and hope that he will settle down.' That was their reaction to everything the Performer did that disturbed them. I knew it had reached gigantic proportions, so I explained to them how Performers operate. I told them that if they didn't like it they couldn't change it, but instead they needed to monitor and accommodate it. They agreed he had an inadequate supply of self-discipline and that they could probably supply the required framework and input of information to monitor what he was doing, but they also agreed that they had not done it so far.

That's the only solution. The Generals expected that one day the Performer would become self-disciplined, and organised – like them. He would not. So, while they continued to expect him to behave in a certain way, he continued to fail them. The problem was made worse because the three Generals never told the Performer the truth. They appeared rather condescending and patronising to him, because they were scared of him. They started being rather manipulative, subtle, dropping hints. Now, Performers are totally heart-motivated, they wear their hearts on their sleeves. Everything comes from the heart — what you see is what you get — and they want and expect to be spoken to honestly, and can't deal with elaborate reasoning or subtle hints, both of which they perceive as verbal manipulation.

If you want to deal with a Performer, tell him the truth straight out, and make your points quickly otherwise he's liable to switch off. Tell him, 'I am frightened of you and I hate it when you behave like this.' They say, 'OK – I can deal with that – let's sort it out.' The problem in the example above was that, as Generals, the partners organised meetings hoping that the situation could be resolved through rational conversation. But, within seconds, the Performer was bored and likely to say, 'If you have something to say, say it and let's get on.'

A General will sit and chat for half-an-hour and at the end of it will suddenly drop a hint of what he is not happy about. Meanwhile the Performer has interrupted or has busied himself taking some phone calls. So, unless someone appreciates why what is happening is happening, there is a chasm — a total lack of understanding of each other. It causes friction and it wastes time.

136

PERFORMERS AS VISIONARIES

Chalkcheese Ltd – taking the problems higher up

Patrick feels very aggrieved after the think-tank meeting with Cliff, the computer expert. He feels his idea to revolutionise the way the company works by installing a new integrated computer system has been hijacked by the others, and that not only will he get no credit for it, but that if they go ahead with the lower-level, cheaper, system A, it won't work as well, and won't fulfil his dream.

In this mood, he has a casual conversation with his boss, the marketing director, Michael. The latter has spoken to Patrick about his innovative ideas several times, and is very interested in them. Michael (who, like Patrick is a Performer-General) is a volatile, intelligent, exuberant type, impatient of rules and formal procedures. When Patrick starts to tell him about the suggested computer system, he's immediately gripped by the idea. Talking about it, Patrick forgets his grievance about the rest of think-tank, and concentrates on his ideas about, and enthusiasm for, system B.

Patrick: So, you see what I mean? This is going to be great for Chalkcheese – it's just what we need to develop much more sophisticated ways of doing things, and to reduce the amount of boring repetitive labour.

Michael: Yes, I think it's really exciting! Right, there's a board meeting tomorrow. I'll bring it up then. No point in hanging around!

We looked at the difference in leadership styles between Performers and Generals in Chapter 3. Performers have an erratic and inspirational style of leadership. They are overtaken by ideas; which envelop them utterly. All they can think of is proceeding towards these ideas, this inspiration. And because they're sociable people, they tell others about it. And because they're charismatic and charming, others are caught up in the enthusiasm and drive, and follow the Performer. They assume that the Performer knows exactly where he is going and precisely the way to get there – neither of which is true. Then, if things start to go wrong, the Performer is blamed for not consulting, not thinking things through, for leading his group into disaster. He's hurt, he had no idea that anything could go wrong – he never intended to damage anyone else, why did they all follow him blindly in the first place?

Power struggles – the armies

As in real-life wars, it's often not the leaders, the instigators of the battles, who lose out or get destroyed. It's the foot-soldiers, the armies, who may not even know what the fighting is about. Individual supporters or whole departments may be axed in an attempt to undermine or isolate one leader in a power struggle. Departments may be given ever more hard-to-reach targets, in order to label them (and their manager) as 'failures'; departments may be understaffed, or underfunded, leading to discontent, destabilisation. Gradually people who become aware that their working lives are not as rewarding and fulfilling as they should be – although they may not be aware of all the reasons for it – start to consider leaving, taking other jobs. Those who can't leave become more and more uncomfortable, new sources of distress flare up, and new conflicts can begin.

137

SUPPORTERS WHO GET SQUASHED

What can people caught up in power games do to distance themselves, protect themselves, or at least make sure their 'side' comes out on top? How can middle management influence the kind of conflicts that happen over their heads, and perhaps shield the people working under them?

Again, we return to the notion of communication, the most powerful Human Technology tool. Let's look again at the Norfolk Medical Centre case that we first examined in Chapter 3 (see page 53).

The Norfolk Medical Centre

The situation there was that a new chief executive (Robert), who was predominantly a Performer, had been appointed with the brief of improving the Centre's profitability. The assistant director (Agnes) was predominantly a General. Their inability to recognise each other's fundamentally different Human Technology types gave rise to many situations of conflict and misunderstanding at senior level. This filtered down to the medical and nursing staff, all of whom felt disenfranchised. They could not understand why traditional practices were suddenly changed without warning. Why project funding that they had relied on for patient-care equipment was suddenly diverted to what they saw as window dressing. All of the staff members had patient care as their top priority, and felt that profitability was secondary, and would in any case come around as a result of good medical practice and results.

There was basically no match between Robert's priorities on the one hand, and Agnes's on the other. Robert's priorities were:

1 Getting attention – primarily from people outside the Centre.
2 Securing positive publicity for the Centre.
3 Improving the Centre's profitability.
4 Having ideas to help him achieve points 1 to 3.

Agnes's priorities were:

1 Ensuring that all staff knew their responsibilities and performed their tasks.
2 The smooth running of the Centre so that patient needs were met.
3 That the Centre made a profit as a result of points 1 and 2.
4 A desire to solve whatever problems she might encounter.

Agnes, the assistant director, who had a lot of knowledge and experience in the workings of the Centre, would try and lay out clear targets and define roles for the staff, telling each one 'Your job is X'. Then Robert, who had some scheme for publicity, or fund-raising, would come in and change it completely; 'Don't do that, do this'. He didn't listen to pleas about the importance of the work that the staff were diverted from. Staff were doing inappropriate work, leaving work undone, becoming unsettled and disillusioned, and many left. This was a real problem, as the Medical Centre was in a relatively remote area, and it was difficult to attract top quality staff. Agnes was very aware of this draining away of what she saw as the Centre's main assets; Robert's attitude was 'Get someone else, don't bother me with it.'

Agnes didn't have the strength to stand up to him. He could always shout her down, and the more she or the other staff complained, the more he felt isolated and embattled. More and more he felt that his efforts were unappreciated, that Agnes and the others were stuck in their ways, that they had no grasp of the real issues. In his mind, improving the profitability of the Medical Centre was crucial to its survival, and the others were refusing to see or accept this.

By itself, a problem like this is insoluble, Someone has to tell the Performer, in a way that reaches him, that his actions are creating chaos. I was called in when everyone realised that the situation was completely out-of-hand. What happened was that Agnes banded together with the finance director, the head of nursing and the operations director. The four together had commonality, and felt comfortable confronting Robert as a group, whereas no one had wanted to act alone. Basically, they said 'We can't go on like this.' When I had talked to everyone there and had a clear picture of what was going on – and what they *thought* was going on, I explained the different Human Technology types to them, and they began to see that their expectations of Robert were never going to be fulfilled. He would never understand why moving technicians off cleaning medical equipment and on to painting the car park could cause the kind of problems and lead to the kind of resentment that it did. Eventually, Robert left the Medical Centre.

The strategy the staff of Norfolk used in this case could be called 'strength in numbers'. However, although they were successful in stopping the conflict situation, at the same time they wasted Robert's talents – he was a great fund-raiser, and could have injected new life into their finances, used, motivated and integrated properly. By the time they decided to do something about the situation it had really deteriorated too far to be retrievable. We talk about some other strategies for 'armies' later in this chapter, some of which can be used before the conflict escalates.

139

MY SIDE AND YOUR SIDE

One big problem in any sort of power struggle is the division of supporters into 'my side and your side'. People who don't *want* to take a side, who don't even feel strongly about the issues, get caught up and aligned with one side or the other. In the 'Norfolk' example above, the nursing and medical staff felt they had to take the side of Agnes, the assistant director, if they were to have their ideas and problems taken into account. Some of them were able to see what Robert was trying to achieve, and might have been able to co-operate with him, if they hadn't felt insecure about their own positions and at the same time felt that they had to be aligned with the people who were concerned about medical standards and patient care – the 'you're either with me or against me' scenario.

This problem of people taking up positions aligned with or against other individuals, groups or departments, can start right at the top. In the case of Flowers and Partners, discussed in Chapters 4 (pp.82–84) and 5 (pp.95–98), an additional problem between the two feuding senior partners was that each had difficulty separating their role of 'managing the company' from their role as 'head of department', and often took up positions representing their 'side' (or department), when they should have been considering the business as a whole.

Each of the senior partners felt that they represented different departments or factions within the partnership. Those departments concerned with new business, sales and so on were the province of the Performer-Soldier; professional services and servicing existing business were represented by the General-Soldier. They were often 'batting for' or defending their own departments rather than considering the partnership as a whole. This was divisive – 'my army' and 'your army', and encouraged an atmosphere of competition rather than co-operation. Where one partner turned all his attention to the areas he knew and specialised in, and the other paid no attention to those parts of the business, a division gradually built up. It started with the thought: 'I don't have to worry about that side of things – so-and-so looks after that'; and developed into a culture of 'My department is more important than his – it must be, because I know nothing about his, but mine is vastly complex and time-consuming.'

When I was called in to help sort out the conflicts between the partners, one of the things that I wanted to do was to make them see how this was affecting the development of the business as a whole – and how the 'armies' were suffering. The 'support troops' felt that members of the other departments were 'enemies', with different goals and objectives. They were confused when departmental agendas seemed to contradict overall corporate agendas, and found it easiest to 'follow the leader', which sometimes meant poor intercompany communication and co-operation.

I therefore worked out a programme with the two senior partners, by which they were encouraged to act proprietarily in favour of the partnership's overall welfare, rather than the welfare of their units within it. So I asked them each to bring two hats to our meetings – on one hat was the label 'Head of My Department' and on the other it said 'Proprietor'. We used to have meetings where, for the first half hour they wore their department hats and looked at issues and problems from a departmental viewpoint, and then for the second half hour I asked them to switch hats. Wearing proprietor hats enabled them to have a completely different view on the issues and problems than they had in the first half of the meeting. They found themselves no longer as adversaries, but able and willing to discuss issues and make decisions on behalf of the whole practice.

Chalkcheese Ltd – the big guns

Gail, Stuart and Natalie have planned their presentation to the board, and agreed to present details of both system A and system B, but to emphasise that in their opinion system A does everything they need, and is their recommendation. When they go to put their presentation on the board agenda, however, they are amazed to hear that the board has already discussed the computer system – the previous week, and the day after the think-tank's last meeting with Cliff Thompson, the computer expert from Tecsol! Michael, the marketing director, who is Patrick's boss, brought it up at the last board meeting, and spoke very persuasively and enthusiastically about the merits of system B.

The rest of the think-tank are confused and angry. Has Patrick been going behind their backs to the board directly? Has he misled Michael about the relative merits of the two systems, since he's so keen on the more expensive system B? And what should they do about it?

Stuart: Look, I don't like this at all. If the board goes for system B, without really knowing all the ins-and-outs, and anything goes wrong – or even if they discover that system A was much cheaper and would do the same basic job, *we'll* be to blame!

Natalie: What do you think we should do?

Stuart: I'll speak to the finance director. He's going to be furious when he finds out that the board's been given half the story – particularly as he thinks Michael the marketing director is a menace, and should never have been appointed. He may have some good ideas, but he's completely disorganised, and always going off on wild goose chases!

141

Gail: Stuart, we don't want to get in the middle of any personal rows between board members! Shouldn't we just put our presentation on the agenda, and explain that although they've heard about it informally already, we are going to give them an in-depth-report?

Natalie: Oh yes, I'm sure that's best – all this going around whispering to people always leads to problems and misunderstandings.

Strategies for those caught in the cross-fire

We saw one strategy earlier in this chapter – 'strength in numbers'. Bonding together, talking about your problems, finding out that others are also feeling insecure and uncertain, stressed by tensions they have no control over and would rather have no part of, can be very reassuring. But in doing so, you are creating what can appear as a threatening force, challenging authority and possibly about to mutiny. This is completely counter-productive. Even in the middle of the most vicious battle, leaders who suspect that their staff are about to stage a revolution will suddenly drop their weapons, and turn about to present an apparently united front against the 'rebels'.

The main strategy for a middleman caught in a senior ding-dong is to tell the truth. 'I need to find out how my job is affected by your row.' Keep querying and questioning; 'What is *my* job?' 'What do you want me to do?' The key is to keep emotional content out of the issue. Lay the problem clearly on the table. 'You have asked me to do X. So-and-so has asked me to do Y. X and Y are incompatible. Please make it clear to me, what I am supposed to do?'

Instead of complaining about what you are not getting, ask for what you want.

Some things to remember:

- find out your role – the grey areas of responsibility are always the weak links in the chain
- get an agenda
- define your personal agenda
- ask for a decision on conflicting instructions
- keep emotion out of discussions – stick to the facts
- try not to take sides
- act as a mirror – 'your row is causing this problem'
- don't participate in whisperings
- keep your integrity (by which I mean your spontaneous honesty) – don't be forced to do things you're not happy about.

The good middle manager in a war zone

Board members and senior management may think they are playing out their power games in private, but in reality everyone is aware that something is going on, and may even know everything about it. What can a good line manager do to help shield the people working for her? First of all, she should take the steps listed in the previous section, avoid becoming ammunition for one person's private vendetta against another. Then, she should concentrate on doing her job thoroughly and competently, which includes the crucial role of empowering staff. Staff should know everything the boss knows. As we said earlier, this can be frightening – the fear is that staff will overtake their boss. But in practice staff respect and like a good manager who clearly sees her role as to empower the people who work under her.

Some key steps to empowering staff:

- share criteria
- share targets

- share rules.

Now, in a power game situation, some of these things may be very hard to achieve. If you are getting conflicting messages and instructions from above, do you pass them down to subordinates unfiltered? Do you pass them on with the acerbic comment, 'These are *today's* targets, no doubt tomorrow's will be different.' No. One of your jobs is to try and act as a buffer, to protect staff from the worst effects of the struggle higher up. If you feel destabilised and out of control, think how insecure they must feel! At the same time, you must not pretend that all is normal. If you are forced to give conflicting instructions from one day to the next, it's important that your staff recognise that this is a problem which is out of your hands, and not either your own whims, or some inadequacy on their part for which they will be blamed.

If you, as manager, have been able to get your role, targets and agenda clearly defined, that's the best protection and security you can give to your staff. If you can pass on guidelines to them which have some backing, then you'll be providing stability and continuity, which is crucial if they are to feel secure and motivated.

143

ISOLATING THE COMBATANTS

Another useful strategy is to make the people playing the power game aware that this is *their* struggle. That no one else is willing to 'take their side'. That they must fight it out alone, and that their battles are not to be allowed to destroy the company in the process.

Chalkcheese Ltd – conflict spreads upwards

The think-tank members are to make their board meeting presentation. Just as they are about to begin, Michael the marketing director, interrupts:

Michael: We talked about this at the last board meeting – no need to go over it again! We can just proceed. Tell Cliff, the computer boffin, to get hold of the gear and let's get on with it.

Gail: I'd still like to present our report to the board. I'm not sure everyone will have a complete picture of all the options, the costs, the targets for the systems, and . . .

Michael: Look, I've already gone over all this, it's a waste of time . . .

At this point Frank, the finance director (and Stuart's boss), speaks up:

Frank: Michael, when you spoke about this subject at the last board meeting, it was not on the agenda, and I for one assumed that you were just giving us a preliminary introduction to the whole idea. We certainly can't make agreements without considering the full implications – particularly the spending implications of the proposal.

Michael: Oh good grief, if you want to go over things again and again . . .

Frank: We are not going over things again. So far we've had no written report, no figures to consider . . .

Stuart: I doubt if you've been told about the different options either!

Chairman: What do you mean? I thought only one system fulfilled the criteria the think-tank agreed on.

Gail: No, please look at page six of the report . . .

Stuart: There are two different systems on offer – one's perfectly adequate for all our needs, and not too expensive, but some people have grandiose ideas about spending ridiculous amounts of money on completely unnecessary frills!

Michael: Now, wait a minute . . .

Patrick: You can't say that – you know Cliff from Tecsol said that in five years time the more expensive system could prove the best investment!

Chairman: Clearly we need to go through the think-tank report in detail. Michael, I really don't think you should have brought this subject up without letting us consider the report first.

WINNING BATTLES AND LOSING WARS

The most dangerous part of any power struggle comes right at the end. When a clear victor emerges, feeling triumphant: 'I've won, I've gained my point, I'm the most powerful one of all' – and looks around at a ruined company, colleagues who no longer like or trust him, customers who won't deal with him, a depleted work-force, the best of whom have left for an easier life elsewhere, he realises that the *war has been lost.*

Power struggles at the top of a business can have this sort of devastating effect. Lower down, they may just result in someone being called in to find out why one area of the business is being so badly disrupted, often involving both parties to the struggle finding themselves out of work.

HANDLING POWER GAMES AND AUTHORITY – A CHECKLIST

■ People see power as a see-saw – if I'm down, you must be up. For me to be up, I've got to get you down.

- Power is not the same as authority. You can have apparent authority without power, and power without official authority.

- Power struggles take place between leaders (people whose predominant personality trait is Performer or General).

- Communication is the key to alleviating the worst effects of power struggles – for both combatants, and those caught up unwillingly.

- Be direct and brief with Performers; be logical and thorough with Generals.

- Strategies for those caught up in power games:
  - open the lines of communication
  - clarify your role
  - define and understand the agendas
  - don't take sides
  - don't get emotional
  - keep your integrity (ie, your spontaneous honesty) and always be professional
  - strength in numbers
  - share criteria
  - share targets
  - share rules
  - isolate the combatants.

145

- In the midst of a battle, never lose sight of the war.

8

Dealing with deadlock

Chalkcheese Ltd – deadlock

Gail is presenting the think-tank report to the board meeting, with some difficulty, as both Frank, the finance director, and Michael, the marketing director, keep interrupting. Both use points from her presentation as springboards for aggressive remarks about each other, about their departments, and about other disagreements in the past. Things are not helped by Patrick and Stuart joining in in support of their respective bosses, and also taking the opportunity to snipe at each other.

Gail: . . . so, as you can see, it's quite a complex and far-reaching proposal. We'd like to suggest that each department consider the report and its recommendations, separately, and then let us have their feedback about how they see the new systems working for them, what sort of implementation problems they foresee, how . . .

Michael: More meetings, more reports, more talk, talk, talk, no *do*! By the time we get around to installing this system, it'll be out of date!

Frank: Typical! That says it all about you . . . rush in, no thought, no consideration, no examination of the implications, no judgement, no balance . . .

Michael: I've had enough of this! What are we talking about here? Computers? Or my ability to do my job?

Frank: If you can't see the link between the two, then you're even more out of touch than I thought!

The Chairman now steps in, saying: Frank, Michael, I think this is an unproductive use of board time. We're not getting anywhere. I propose that we circulate the report as Gail suggested, and that I meet with the two of you to discuss this amongst ourselves before the next board meeting.

Sometimes it is just not possible to avoid a head-on collision with people, however much you may wish to get around it, and the result can be deadlock. But there are ways to deal with deadlock. This chapter explains some of the techniques and shows how it is possible to move the seemingly immovable.

Negotiating out of deadlock

Once a conflict situation appears to be deadlocked, it may seem too late for negotiation. This is not so – the problem is the way we have conventionally gone about the business of negotiation. One pattern is to simply state baldly, 'What I want is . . .', and to offer no awareness of the needs or wants of other parties, and to show no flexibility. Now, this may seem like no negotiation at all – but some people consider it 'putting all their cards on the table, keeping nothing back and, stating their objectives clearly'. Another pattern is for each side to wildly overstate their objectives or understate their offers, and to keep to themselves the real level at which they would be happy to settle. Then they only move from these positions in response to a movement from the other side, or to threats from the other side to withdraw from the negotiation completely.

Both these ways of opening negotiations are counter-productive, and divisive. They close more doors than they open and are almost certain to result in a settlement which at best leaves one side feeling aggrieved and hard done by, and at worst has this effect on both sides! At the same time, an atmosphere of opposition, of combat, is created and established, both parties becoming accustomed to dealing with each other on an adversarial basis.

The key to successful negotiation is to start from the basis of what parties have in common. This is true for negotiations between individuals, representatives of departments, interest groups or corporations, and also for negotiations in which there are several concerned parties or just two. There must be some reason *why* the negotiation is taking place at all – you must have some common ground. You could be partners or colleagues, employee and employer, producer and seller, customer and supplier, even representatives of competing companies in the same marketplace. If you had no common interest, there could be no conflict, and no negotiation.

> **You are either part of the problem or part of the solution: you cannot be in no-man's-land.**

SIFTING THE ISSUES TO ESTABLISH THE COMMON OBJECTIVE

The first step in any negotiation should be to agree on an aim for the negotiation based on common interests, not on opposing positions. Here are some examples of stated positions and the kinds of common goal that might be set when negotiating:

Example 1

Sales director: We want product information three months before release so that we can take it to the marketplace.

Production director: We don't want to release product information until we've tested prototypes, in case we make major design changes.

Common interest: To make sure the marketplace is fully and accurately informed about a product immediately it is available, avoiding expensive delay between release and sales.

Example 2

Junior partner: My partnership revenue is based on my experience and customer list when I joined. Now I'm bringing in much more work and lots of new clients. I want a bigger share.

Senior partner: Giving you a bigger share means giving everyone else a smaller share, and I'm not willing to take a smaller share.

Common interest: Increasing the overall profitability of the partnership.

Example 3

Employees' representative: Now that the company has increased in size, we want an agreed structure of salaries and increases – some people are getting much less than others for the same job.

Management representative: We want to be able to reward special efforts, creativity, loyalty and long service, and not to be tied to some artificial rewards structure.

Common interest: To pay employees what they see as a fair level of reward, so that they continue to do their best for the company.

UNCOVERING THE REAL ISSUES

A problem in negotiation of difficult or deadlocked situations is that the apparent difficulty – what people are arguing about – is often only the tip of the disagreement. It may be the only thing people in conflict are prepared to argue about, as the real causes are too painful, and they prefer to throw up a smoke-screen rather than try to argue their actual case. This can make it very hard for opponents to understand why their best efforts to offer compromise, to reach a mutually beneficial agreement, are turned down. They don't know that the real agenda is still hidden from them, and that they are somehow expected to deduce the actual causes and to offer compromises and concessions on those as well.

People may also think that being secretive about their real goals is a good negotiating ploy. They may see it as 'holding their cards close to their chest'; thinking, 'I won't tell them. I don't care about giving way on that, I'll pretend I do, in case I need it to win a trick later on. I won't give that away, I may need to trade it for something I want.' This sort of thinking results in obscuring the real motives and goals of opponents, making it difficult to identify where the real point of conflict is, and therefore to isolate and deal with it.

Let's look at a company I worked with recently, where the people involved found it particularly difficult to come out and state what they really felt and what they wanted, where the actual nature of the conflict was unclear, and no one was quite sure of what the common corporate goals actually were.

Beanstalk the Builders – the characters and the scenario

Jack Beanstalk founded the company 39 years ago. It's a building construction enterprise with a turnover of £175 million per annum and 800 employees. Jack has two children, Ben and Jen – both in their 30s, with Jen the elder. Both children went to university, although academia was always a struggle for Ben.

149

Jack is domineering, autocratic, explosive, manages by crisis, and is always putting out fires. He seems to know everybody and thinks he knows everything. During his stewardship the company's fortunes have lurched a lot and, on three occasions, it almost sank. Its current situation is that, having barely survived the recession, it is only just about breaking even. Jack has run the business through yes-men and yes-women – if they agreed with him, they could stay, if they disagreed, they were out. Jack makes all the major decisions himself, in an autocratic and dictatorial manner.

Ben's approach is different to Jack's. He's more right brain, more creative, artistic, charismatic and unstructured. He explodes more readily than his father and, as result, most people steer clear of him. Ben's expertise is in computer technology, but the marriage of advanced technology and the building trade has yet to be established, so it's not always clear how his expertise can be utilised by the company. Jen's behavioural characteristics are more like those of her father – left brain, tending towards the structured, organised and methodical, rather than the 'firework' style of Ben.

The business is privately owned by the family, with the equity divided between Jack and his children. Both Ben and Jen have notional titles and jobs within the business. Jack, who is in his 60s, wants to withdraw from day-to-day activities, but he doesn't feel enough trust or confidence in Ben to turn the running of the business over to him. Over the past ten years he has employed a series of chief executive officers to manage the company, on the understanding that they report to Jack, who maintains the right to veto any decision at whatever level. All these appointments proved singularly unsuccessful – anyone who suggested anything Jack didn't like was shot down, and the remainder brought no new ideas into the company and were unable to prevent Jack making potentially disastrous decisions.

In Human Technology terms, Jack is a four-star General. He expects things done his way – to get on with him you can be a mere one-, two-, or three-star General, but you must be a General, you must be authoritarian, rule-based, follow in the 'way things have always been done' – and you must be subservient to Jack, the four-star General. Ben simply isn't like that. He's predominantly a Performer who has sudden bright ideas, which may involve new things the company has never considered before. He has poor communication skills which he, and those around him, find frustrating and ineffective (he is good at telling stories but not at presenting the facts of a situation). For the most part he operates outside the sparse company rules, regulations and procedures – particularly in relation to issues involving expenditure on 'necessary' equipment.

This unmethodical, unregulated way of behaving is a constant source of exasperation and irritation to Jen, particularly as Jack (by not saying anything) seems to condone it. Jen is coherent, structured, concise and authoritative. Her role and function are vague and loosely defined. She is married with two young children and works part-time. At the time I first began to work with Beanstalk's she was so disillusioned with the way things were going that she was talking about withdrawing from the business, simply taking an income or flat payment from it, but not getting involved day to day any longer, and possibly even moving abroad with her family.

Ben and Jen don't have rows at work, but neither do they co-operate with each other, let alone join forces to try and resolve the problems facing the business. They tend to suppress their disagreements rather than try to air and solve them.

Jack's major problem is that, beyond arguing and shouting, he does not have a social, or even business, relationship with either of his children. As the years have progressed, this has become ever more painful, especially with the advent of grandchildren. This is deeply distressing to his wife, Ben and Jen's mother, who has seen her family divided and business arguments brought into every social and family occasion, making it impossible to retain any close relationship with her children and grandchildren.

The family conflict (usually emotional in nature) was impacting adversely on the business, causing noticeable financial difficulty. In order to deal with this impasse, a forum for discussion had to be created so that the problems could be talked out and talked through. In the first place the family needed to set some common goals – some things that they all agreed were worth striving for.

The stances

To summarise, at the start of negotiation the positions were as follows:

150

Jack

- wants to retire from day-to-day business, handing over to someone else
- doesn't see Ben as competent – 'He doesn't do things the way I do them'
- doesn't see Jen as committed to the business
- has a poor opinion of non-family managers
- wants to defuse business tensions and rebuild family relationships.

Ben

- wants to take on running the company
- wants to get out from his father's authoritarian rule
- wants to make changes and run things his own way
- wants to use non-family managers to run day-to-day business, and to take the 'Chairman' role himself
- wants to defuse business tensions and rebuild family relationships.

Jen

- wants to withdraw from the conflicts of the business – ie, between Jack and Ben
- wants to retain an income and job from the business
- doesn't like or respect Ben's management style
- thinks Jack has been soft on Ben's 'unprofessional' methods and undisciplined approach
- like Jack, distrusts non-family managers
- wants to defuse business tensions and rebuild family relationships.

151

One common goal is immediately obvious – all three agree that their cohesiveness as a family is being destroyed by conflict within the business. They all agreed that they wanted an end to the negotiation – an end which did not include alienation of any of the three participants. They wanted to be able to spend Christmas together, to have the grandchildren visit their grandparents with their parents, to have their spouses become friends. So any end to the negotiation which envisaged one or more party feeling hurt, excluded or aggrieved was unacceptable – the consequences to the family would be too damaging even if the business itself were to benefit.

So, having agreed that, they could then set other common goals that did not conflict with the family goal. For example, they might have decided that what they all wanted was to take the family out of the business, by selling it, ideally giving Jack plenty of money with which to retire comfortably, Ben enough capital to start something new and Jen an investment income sufficient for herself and her family. But when they looked at that option they all agreed that the time was not right for selling the business (it was not doing as well as it might at that time, and overall economic conditions were not ideal for a sale), and that it would be to their mutual benefit it if were to continue with their involvement. Ben and Jen were also surprised to discover, when they started to think and talk about it, how committed they both felt to Beanstalk's, and how much they wanted it to carry on.

This then made a number of questions quite clear, and helped to focus the negotiating process on the need to find answers to these:

- What would the management structure of the company be when Jack retired from day-to-day management?
- How much authority would Jack retain, and how would it be limited?
- What would the involvement of Ben and Jen be following Jack's retirement?
- What financial provisions would be made for each family member?
- What would they have to do (if anything) to earn this money?

Goal setting and personal agendas

After setting some goals for the Beanstalk negotiation – what do we want to achieve? And when? I proceeded to get the combatants to set their own goals, to think about what they wanted personally. I tried to get them to separate 'I deserve . . . I've earned . . . If I went elsewhere I'd get . . .' from what they would find satisfying in the long term.

I had many conversations with Jack, Jack and his wife, Jen and Ben. In Jack's case I established that his goal was to remove himself from the day-to-day running of the company, that he deeply desired that the business continued, succeeded and regained its former profitability, but that his struggle was letting go of the idea that Beanstalk's was his own private business. He had structured the organisation with himself at the top, all-powerful. As a result, the board of directors felt powerless and decided not to take major or difficult decisions. Jack admitted (at first privately) that he could not bring himself to let go because there was no one good enough to take over.

All the previous CEOs had been given the impossible task of running a £175 million turnover company, while reporting to someone who demanded and exercised a veto on their decisions and overruled their authority. Jack agreed that at some point he would *have* to put his faith and trust in another.

In my talks with Ben, he said that ultimately he would like to have actual control of the business, but acknowledged that he wasn't ready at the moment. Right now, he would only want to manage by consensus, surrounding himself with experts for support. His main problem with his father was the latter's almost complete lack of consultation on either business or family issues. The subject of succession was a non-starter between them, and the entire organisation was aware of this. Ben foresaw his birthright disappearing due to his insecurity, lack of confidence, his explosive nature and his inarticulateness. He blamed his father for not being different and felt that relations with both his father and Jen were stretched to breaking point.

Ben summarised his choices as being between selling the company (not much chance at present); leaving (but to do what?); or facing up to his father and resolving the succession problem. Ben chose to try the last option.

Having initially told me that she wanted to leave Beanstalk's and was more concerned with her husband and children, Jen actually revealed more of her own position after we'd talked a few times. She eventually said that, if the truth be known, she really wanted to pursue her career – ideally at Beanstalk's, but she had some conditions. First, she only wanted to stay on if she was genuinely wanted by the board of directors; and secondly, only if she had a proper role with accountability and responsibilities.

She found Ben too difficult and unstructured in his dealings to establish any meaningful relationship, socially or commercially. However, she also thought that the way forward was identical to that favoured by Ben – to resolve the succession issue. She knew that her mother was desperately unhappy with Jack's dilemma and the current hostility. Jen wanted a quality management structure that would boost the organisation's asset value and bring stability to a fluid situation.

So, even in thinking about, and in talking to an independent third party about their personal goals, agendas and problems, the combatants had clarified the negotiations, and sometimes had even moved from their original positions.

153

Changing your goals

Goals can change with changes in circumstances. We talked in Chapter 6 about the relationship between pain and change, and the need for some degree of change throughout life. The people in the Beanstalk case are classic examples of individuals hurting themselves through their refusal to face up to and accept change, and the need for change. Jen, for example, would not even admit to herself that she was so unhappy with the situation that she was considering pulling out of something very important to her, and to which she thought she might have a real contribution to make. But as soon as the situation was altered by every-one admitting the need for change, she found it easier to accept and talk about her own agenda and potential contribution. Initially she could only see the way out of her pain, the way to change, through cutting loose from Beanstalk's, but as Jack and Ben began to talk about change, it opened up the possibility for her to change *within* the company.

Know and accept your own limits

How far are you really prepared to push, or to retreat? At what point will you give up altogether? We talked about 'keeping your integrity' in Chapter 7 when we were looking at being caught up in power games. The same consideration comes up when negotiating in a deadlock situation. It's up to you to establish your own outer limits. Do you really have the power to insist on more money? More authority? More staff? As an employee, you will always have to keep in mind that however reasonable your demands appear to you, you may not achieve them, because you simply haven't got the bargaining power to push them through. In that case, what are you prepared to accept as a minimum? Will you leave if you don't get all of what you want? Half of what you want? 90 per cent?

These sort of decisions – taken between a rock and a hard place – come up much more frequently if you don't follow the rule about keeping the common interest in mind, and negotiating from that goal rather than from your own agenda. When you put people on the spot – 'Give me what I ask for, or I'm off ' – that's a direct challenge. They may want to give you what you've asked for, but in confronting them that way, you are making a direct power bid – giving you what you want also means giving you the power to repeat the demand.

154   In the Beanstalk situation, for example, Jack, who was unwilling to hand over to anyone he didn't think good enough, and never would think that anyone other than himself was good enough, recognised that because of his age he was going to have to back down from the authoritarian 'dictator' position he'd occupied for so long. The alternative was that he struggled on, feeling more and more exhausted by the effort required, and the company would gradually dwindle and fail. The only possibility for the company he built to continue on without him was for him to hand over in an organised and planned fashion.

Before I became involved as the mediator in the Beanstalk situation, Jen felt she had reached the end of her tether – she was getting out. Even when she began to see some hope of change, she stated her limits very clearly – she would only stay with the company if she could be really useful; she was not prepared to be a token manager/executive.

Removing the personal

We looked at the need to take the personal, the emotional, out of the communication process in Chapter 6. This is even more important in a deadlock situation. The 'common interest' goal must always be to the forefront – there is really no place for hurt feelings, damaged egos or insecurities. It is the responsibility of everyone in the negotiation to try and calm emotional situations, to defuse person-person tensions. It is a fallacy that everything said in the extremes of emotion carries an element of truth. If you look back at Chapter 2, you'll see how the different parts of our persona push us in different directions, and can make us do or say things that in calmer moments we would think twice about.

> **I add suffering to the world just as much when I take offence as when I give offence.**

Negotiations in a deadlock situation should not take place if the participants:

- feel tired, hungry or stressed
- are in an unfamiliar situation
- are liable to interruptions
- feel constrained by the presence of others
- have had too much to drink
- feel insecure because of the venue or because they are unprepared.

155

The Beanstalk situation illustrates how difficult it is to separate personal agendas, emotions and relationships from business ones. In that situation there is the extra dimension of the family being involved in the business, and this extra dimension, this overlay, often takes priority over the dynamic of running the business. It is very difficult for a son to live up to the expectations of a father, for example, particularly as these expectations are rarely voiced – they are subtle, subversive and can form a great barrier between the two components of the dynamic. The way forward in family business conflicts is not so different from that of any other business conflicts. It is to recognise that as well as the personal and business goals and personal and business agendas, which need to be clarified and communicated, there are also family goals and agendas. People may be used to taking particular roles within the family – and happy to do so – but find that these roles don't translate to the business, and that they don't want to play the same parts in a business context. Just like telling people that they need to be clear whether they are wearing their 'owner of the company' hat or their 'head of my department' hat, participants in a family business need to know whether they are acting as, for example 'Daddy's clever little daughter' or 'assistant sales director'.

Chalkcheese Ltd – the Chairman acts

The day after the board discussed the think-tank report, the Chairman arranges a private meeting with Frank (the finance director) and Michael (the marketing director).

Chairman: Frank, Michael, I'm concerned about the conflicts between you two. Yesterday's meeting was turned into a battlefield between you, when really it was about a straightforward, non-controversial report presentation. This situation has been escalating for months, and I can see your personal animosities filtering down into your departments. I even noticed in the meeting that the people from accounts and marketing were obviously at odds. I doubt they'd have allowed that to be so plain at a board meeting, if they didn't feel they had support from the top – you two.

Michael: I may get a bit excited at times, and perhaps I'm a bit more forthright than people like. But I'm worried that Chalkcheese could be left behind in the fast-paced world of today, and that the slow ponderous way we do things is holding us back – we're missing opportunities.

Frank: I suppose by that you mean that *I* am holding us back . . .

Chairman: Now, there's my point – I really think this has gone far enough! I've heard good reports about the work of a management consultant called Martin C who specialises in resolving conflicts of this sort, and I want you both to see him. Settling all the issues will probably take time, but let's make a start. There's a risk the company will suffer unless we can begin to get this sorted out.

Difficult people

Some people find it easy to enter into and come out of rows – they positively enjoy them. They almost feel that unless everyone has had a good shout/cry/thumping, nothing has been resolved. These people can be extremely difficult to deal with if you are not someone who copes well with vocal arguments. Many people simply walk away from this sort of row – they refuse to participate because they so dislike the emotional reactions within themselves. This means that the perpetrators of the row feel they've 'won'. They'll do it again and again – it's a successful negotiating tactic, isn't it?

Dealing with these people means learning to deal with their anger, their emotional outbursts. You have to refuse to participate in shouting matches, slinging insults and bullying.

The message put out is the message received.

But you must not walk away from the negotiations either. Make sure that before you enter a negotiating session with a difficult person that you have all the points about your agenda, your limits and your common interest quite clear in your mind. Be very direct, clear, and brief in what you say. Remember that Performers, who are often the people who will happily bluster and rage at their opposition, have poor listening skills and a short attention span. They are also quick to take personal offence if they see themselves as being challenged or denigrated. If your opponent starts shouting, speak quietly and calmly. Tell them directly that you find it hard to deal with them when they respond in this angry manner. Remind them of the common goals of negotiation. If they carry on, suggest a few minutes break to cool off. If they are still loud and unpleasant, suggest that you postpone the meeting until a future date. But don't walk out without a time, date and venue set for that next meeting, because that too feeds the idea that you can be overborne by emotional, bullying tactics.

The only way to defuse emotion is to acknowledge it – eg, 'You seem very angry about this' or, 'You seem really upset about that'. Always state the truth of the issue.

Memories 157

Negotiations are about the present and the future. Before negotiations can take place, however, it may be necessary to deal with 'unfinished business' that pulls the parties back into the past. This clearing of the decks allows attention to be focused on present and future business.

Certainly the present situation may have been reached through a whole catalogue of past 'wrongs', but what you have to deal with here and now is how to get the current situation right, and keep on improving it. In the Beanstalk case, for example, Jack and Ben will get nowhere if they harp on each other's past mistakes – Jack continuing to list off Ben's errors of judgement, bad budget control, rows with staff, or Ben continuing to complain that Jack has always overruled him, insisted on things being done 'Jack's way'. Once they have admitted to themselves and each other what sort of people they are, and how their Human Technology typology affect the way they've behaved in the past, then that's it. Jack *is* authoritarian, dictatorial and has trouble delegating; Ben *is* volatile, emotional and a poor communicator. Now the question is, how can those behavioural characteristics be coped with and taken into account when negotiating a new relationship for the future?

Mediation

My role in the discussions with Beanstalk's was that of professional mediator. There's a saying about ways of solving disputes: 'There is arbitration, there is litigation, there is liquidation or there is mediation.'

The legal culture to a significant extent is based on adversarial principles, and the aim of litigation, of lawyers, is to 'win'. The assumption is always that there is a wrong-doer, that a hurt has been committed, that one party has been damaged by the other, and that the solution involves some sort of restitution, some transfer of money or power from one side to the other.

Arbitration has similarities to litigation – opponents present their case and an outside judge chooses between them. The difference is that the parties involved select an agreed arbitrator, and the process is probably cheaper and rather more flexible and private than litigation. However, it can still result in a 'win-lose' situation, where one party could feel hard done by or feel that the other has gained unfairly. It is the arbitrator who assesses the 'cases' of the opponents, and makes the ruling.

158

In a commercial context, relationships should not be adversarial – rather they should be co-operative. We have more to gain long term by supporting each other than from knocking each other down. Conflict resolutions should be on a win-win basis – 'I gain/retain something without loss of face, you gain/retain something without loss of face. We both gain or retain respect and understanding for each other. Maybe we don't get exactly what we wanted, or thought we wanted, at the start of the process, but at the end of the process neither of us feels that we've been 'done'.

Professional mediation is not much known in the UK as yet. It is more usual in the USA. As we saw in Chapter 4, the USA is a country of Performers, and also one of the most litigious societies in the world. At the same time as holding the attitude that rules and regulations are there to be broken, people will also litigate at the drop of a hat, for huge sums of money.

About 15 years ago, the chairmen of two large New York-based conglomerates were locked into a dispute. The usual procedure would be to get an army of lawyers, go to court, fight it out, pay out huge costs, and a huge settlement. Expensive and very divisive. The chairmen, who knew each other, wanted to settle the dispute, but knew that they and their companies were going to have to continue dealing with each other, so they went to their lawyers and asked 'Is there any other way?' Their lawyers told them about a system being used in California, called mediation, where people try and talk things out rather than fight them out. The two chairmen called in some mediators. It worked very successfully, they settled their dispute relatively quickly, cheaply and privately, but more important, to their minds, was the fact that they were able to carry on working in the same marketplace without bitterness, and as friends. At that time mediation became more formally established as an alternative tool for resolving business disputes.

One advantage of mediation is that the mediators don't have a vote on what the outcome should be. When you mediate you put on the table the personalities involved and the expectations people have of each other. The law has a very small role to play, it's not a case of 'this is the legal solution', it's more about what the two opponents would have wanted. The opponents select the solution themselves. It is not a closed offer, and the mediators themselves make no ruling. They might make suggestions, might make each side look at the strengths or weaknesses, points of contact with the other side. A mediator might say to one opponent, 'What do you think are the strengths of the other person's case? What do you think they really want? How far could you go towards satisfying those requirements?' Then the mediator would go to the other side and try and find out the same sort of information. The mediator wouldn't disclose one side's information or thinking to the other side without express permission. Their role is more to helping each side identify for themselves what compromise or middle route they'd be prepared to follow. The mediator assists the opposing parties to design their own solution. The solution is *theirs*, not imposed by outside forces. It takes into full account the personalities involved and the commercial reality of the situation, but the legal perspective comes out very low down the list of priorities.

159

Mediation is a process of interposing between parties, as a friend of each, in order to find common ground so that a mutually acceptable solution can be reached. It is private, confidential, and the outside world never needs to know that a dispute has taken place. In a large corporation, it might even be possible to shield staff members, and prevent the kind of destabilisation talked about in Chapter 7. The process of reaching a mutual understanding is just that – it allows each side to gain knowledge of each others's stances, needs and aims, and to restate and reanalyse their own. Their own input into the solution means that they have time to digest and get to grips with the stages of it, nothing comes like a bolt from the blue. It provides a basis for future communication and co-operation – particularly important when the dispute is within-company, and people have to continue to work together. And it's much cheaper than going to law!

Business should be a community endeavour to be enjoyed and relished by all. Most businesses understand the necessity of preserving stable and harmonious relationships with clients and customers during the course of normal commercial activity. In the event of a dispute, swiftness, together with the low key approach of the mediation process can allow the continuity of communication required to avoid any stalemate in business activity. Mediators operate with the understanding that all information communicated is on the basis of confidentiality. Their functions include:

- defining the corporate culture
- facilitating communications between people
- converting dominating directors into effective leaders
- designing career paths both for junior and senior partners
- convening a forum to facilitate problem resolution
- developing consensus from conflict
- interpreting personal goals in relation to the corporate agenda
- mediating impasses to avert disputes.

Some corporate mediation specialists often try for a fast resolution of corporate disputes. The mediator has, say, two days to come up with a solution that the opponents and their lawyers haven't suggested so far. In disputes which are rooted in conflicts between people, this is not always as effective as a rather slower process can be. There is often a lot of left-over emotional anger, and feelings of dissatisfaction: 'Well, it was midnight, we'd reached the deadline, so we had to sign the agreement, but really, this was still outstanding, I don't think we resolved that, such and such wasn't really fair . . .' In a dispute like the Beanstalk problem, which was all about people, with the additional complication that they were closely related to each other and wanted to improve and continue their family and social relationship as well as their business one, I think it takes longer than a few days – meetings need to be spread over several weeks and months, giving people time to come to terms with the need for change – change within themselves and in their attitude to the problems.

THE BEANSTALK MEDIATION

When trying to act as mediator for the Beanstalk family, I started by getting each member of the family to talk to me about their personal goals, and what they saw as the company goals. Following that series of conversations, I decided to try and heal the rift between Ben and Jen, as in all probability they would someday assume ownership of the business.

By explaining to them both the different personality types involved, I hoped to create a greater understanding of themselves, each other, their natural skills, and, most importantly, their shortcomings. Ben then recognised the left-brain, structured, methodical and, at times, autocratic approach of Jen. In the same way, Jen recognised the creative, firework, new ideas and expansionist approach of Ben.

I led a number of sessions with Jen and Ben, and over time they grew into mutual respect, and it was possible to draw up a business strategy and plan that suited them both. Over a five to six-month period normal (if rather guarded) relations were established, and problems started to be resolved. Ben and Jen are basically devoted to the family business and have an intense desire for its survival and increased profitability.

Simultaneously, I was discussing with Jack, and with Jack and his wife, the qualities of Ben and Jen. Jack admitted that he had ruled by a divide and conquer strategy that formed a wedge between the children. He had used this for so long that even when it created a rift at a social level he felt unable to change. Jack also admitted that he enjoyed and perhaps needed the power, control and status of his authority, held on to for so many years. It was almost a relief, he said, to consider relinquishing this authority, and was delighted that at long last his children had demonstrated to him their capability to take on responsibility, decision making and, more crucially, to stand up to him. Jack's wife played a key role in acting as a conduit, and I had many conversations with her with that in mind.

Eventually, I chaired a meeting with the entire family, together with the business's financial adviser at which they constructed an outline of a 'family constitution'. This document included guidelines on how the firm and family were to deal with (and the time period of) Jack's succession; the roles, responsibilities and accountability of Jack, Ben and Jen; the remuneration of the family; what roles they had to perform to receive this remuneration; how to resolve emotional outbursts; how to keep family (as opposed to business) problems in check; and dates for regular 'family council' meetings to discuss progress.

161

To ensure the requisite managerial skills, and for business continuity, Jen and Ben agreed that they would have no more role in line management. An external managing director would be found to run the existing team and to select a non-executive director to further dilute the previous autocratic and emotional regime. Meanwhile, Jack agreed to become 'Life Chairman' but with no day-to-day managerial functions.

CLARIFYING WHO'S INVOLVED

In most negotiations there are a few key participants – in the Beanstalk case, for example, Jack, Ben and Jen were clearly the key players. But there are other people who have to play their parts and must be considered in any negotiation. Jack's wife played a crucial role in helping the others to accept the idea of a mediator, and in acting as a communication conduit. Because her main concern was to improve the family relationship, when things got difficult she helped to bring them back to the common good of not allowing the business to break up the family. But she was not included in business discussions and didn't give her opinion on how things should be resolved. She acted as a supporter, a catalyst, and a 'friend' to all the main players.

Another person who acted as catalyst and conduit was the business's financial adviser, an older individual that all the family knew well and respected. He was able to give the 'company' input in the same way that Jack's wife was able to give the 'family' input. He could concentrate on what the business needed for its development and well being, and defuse emotional disputes by bringing the participants back to a consideration of what was best for the business first, and how they could act to bring it about.

Also involved were the non-family managers currently employed by Beanstalk, and those who were considered and interviewed for future management positions. It was vital that such players were not destabilised by involving them at every stage of the negotiations, but that their abilities, willingness to perform in the roles requested of them and commitment to Beanstalk's was considered. Once it became clear that a non-family managing director and a group of line managers were to be employed as core management for Beanstalk's, and what their responsibilities were to be, they had to be brought into discussions. It was important that they had a real understanding of how things were to work, how far their rights and responsibilities stretched, and what their relationships to the family members were to be.

162

Chalkcheese Ltd – moving out of deadlock

The marketing and finance directors, Michael and Frank, agree to discuss their differences with Martin C, the management consultant.

Martin comes to visit them at Chalkcheese two days later. He talks to each separately and explains the Human Technology system – very much as he did when helping Gail with her early problems with the think-tank members.

After some soul-searching the mediation is successful and the two directors come to realise that the feud between them has been souring company relationships at every level, and causing problems for other directors and staff. Michael and Frank agree to co-operate over the think-tank report as the first step in their new working relationship. They decide to wait for the department feedback on the report, which the chairman asked to be circulated, but to try and come to a very speedy decision about the installation of the new computer system once the comments are in.

DEALING WITH DEADLOCK – A CHECKLIST

- Negotiation is the only way out of deadlock.

- Negotiation should start by finding the common interest: 'What do we both want to gain at the end of this negotiation?'

- Be prepared to state your real opinions, feelings, agenda and goals – holding them back because they are too painful, or as a negotiating ploy, makes it harder for your opponent to give you what you want.

- The aim in a Beanstalk-type negotiation is not to beat your opponent – it is to achieve a mutually satisfying conclusion.

- Goals and agendas can change during negotiation – as people find out more about their opponents' positions and interests, they may be able to move from their first stances.

- Define your own limits. Know how far you are prepared to go, how much you care about a particular point.

- Don't allow difficult people to bully you by shouting and making scenes. Don't shout and make scenes yourself.

163

- Don't let past grievances dominate negotiations. Negotiation should relate to the present and the future.

- Mediation helps the opposing parties to come to their own solution, rather than having one imposed on them.

9

Creating effective teams

Chalkcheese Ltd – resolution

An early date has been set for department feedback on the think-tank report. Only a fortnight later, the board of directors meets again.

Chairman: I'm delighted to see such an enthusiastic response to the report on the proposed new computer installation. I know that Frank and Michael have been doing some work on the departmental comments – Michael would you like to speak about these?

Michael: Yes, thank you. I've met with the department heads, and with the outside computer consultant. The department heads, while enthusiastic about the new integrated system, were all rather nervous about the more sophisticated 'system B'. They were worried about how to move off the mainly manual systems they are currently using, into making full use of the new system, without disrupting normal working too seriously.

So I asked the computer consultant to meet with us, and he suggested a series of stages for the transition, allowing sub-systems to be installed one bit at a time. That way only part of the office need be disturbed at any one time, and only a few people need be away being trained. No part of the company need be out of operation for more than two days at most. This sort of step-by-step installation is much easier and more efficient with the more sophisticated system B, which is the reason the managers were keen on that, rather than system A. As you may recall, I have always preferred system B, as being more flexible in the long run, and offering more opportunities for new uses immediately.

Frank: I had been worried about the cost implications of system B, which, if you look at just the buying-in price as a whole, is a lot more expensive than system A. But after this round of consultations, and the suggestion that the system be introduced one part at a time, the financial picture looks quite different.

Partly, it's because the cost can be spread across two or even three financial years, without significantly holding up the planned installation. And partly, with the smaller disruption in the day-to-day running of the company and the savings we can expect to make with greater efficiency, the hidden costs of system B are lower. So I am also recommending system B.

Chairman: Are there any questions other board members would like to raise at this stage?

15 minutes later

Chairman: Let's now take a vote on what we should do ... OK, that's unanimous in favour of system B.

If you really want to prevent conflict in your organisation, one of the best ways is to make sure you have compatible people on board in the first place. This chapter looks at ensuring the right mix of personalities in order to form a co-operative and productive team; and at how to encourage good team integration.

What is a team?

'Team' is a word that means lots of different things. It can mean 'side', as in 'my side' and 'your side', and imply competition with the outside, inner support and integration. In current management parlance it often refers to small interdepartment workgroups of individuals with different skills who come together to work on a single project or group of projects.

165

Basically, a workplace 'team' is any group of individuals with a goal or goals in common, sometimes from the same department, sometimes from different departments, sometimes including people from different levels of the corporate hierarchy and sometimes even including non-company personnel. Even regular suppliers and customers can be thought of as part of the 'team' in certain industries.

Teams divide into the formal and the informal. Formal teams are recognised and set up by the company to fulfil a certain role. They usually have a name, an official head, specific jobs to do, a well-defined structure and a predetermined relationship with other formal company teams.

Informal teams may be subdivisions of formal teams, arising from the overlap between two or more teams, or may have no relations to formal teams at all. Often informal teams are formed on a social basis – people who do things like regularly going to the pub together, playing tennis together, or reading each other's horoscopes! Informal teams develop their own rules, hierarchies and cultures. Like formal groups they usually have a leader, but of course this person is not appointed or 'labelled' as such.

A person may be both a 'formal' team leader and an 'informal' team leader. The charismatic, dynamic small company boss could easily also be the role model when it comes to company socialising, and the formal and informal leadership roles are certainly not mutually exclusive. This is particularly true of a leader who feels happiest when surrounded by loyal supporters – they will both recruit and make friends of people who are happy to 'be in their gang'.

The informal team, and its leader, have real power. An informal leader, unrecognised by authority, with no particular title or corporate responsibilities, may be able to dictate, or at least strongly influence, subtle but all-important aspects of corporate life such as the company culture and rhythm (discussed later in this chapter).

Both formal and informal teams can be characterised by having:

- *fences:* you can be in – or out;
- *rules:* if you don't follow them – you're out (for formal groups, these are – or should be – explicit; for informal teams they are unwritten);
- *codes:* if you are in, you know them – if you're out, you don't;
- *pressure to conform:* in the formal team this may be the official threat of sacking or demotion if you don't follow the rules or, more generally, subscribe to team standards; in both the informal *and* the formal team it may consist of the human desire to belong, to be liked, to fit in.
- *punishments:* in both formal and informal groups these tend to be progressive – rarely do you see 'one offence and you're out'. However, in both groups the succession of punishments tend to be remarkably similar – starting with an unspoken atmosphere of disapproval, then an overt expression of disapproval, followed by the removal of privileges, suspension and expulsion. An example is set out in Table 9.1.

HOW GOOD IS YOUR TEAM?

A good team is better than the sum of its individual members. Team members give each other support, inspiration and a sense of belonging. There is an exchange of skills and knowledge, where personal ambitions fit into team achievements, and a feeling of bonding and pride in the team and its day-to-day activities is created. A good team should be more productive and effective than a team where its members work as unconnected individual 'cogs', and much more so than a team where the members are all rubbing against each other and causing friction.

As before, the oil that smooths the friction between team members is quality communication. It is crucial that the objectives of the team are clearly stated and understood by everyone. All members must feel able to give their views honestly and to express their reservations, without fear of comeback. Much of the team atmosphere is dependent on how well the team leader fulfils his or her role, which we'll look at below.

166

Table 9.1

Formal	Informal
Tom is repeatedly a few minutes (five to ten) late for work.	Sam arranges to go bowling with a group from work every Friday, but is often late or doesn't turn up.
Unspoken disapproval Maria, his department head, begins to express her disapproval by looking pointedly at her watch when he arrives, and asking if he's had transport problems.	Brian, the person who books the bowling alley, begins to express his disapproval by looking pointedly at his watch when Sam arrives, and comments such as 'Nice of you to give us your time, Sam!'
Overt disapproval A few weeks later, she stops him on the way into the office and says 'Tom, everyone else manages to make it in by 9.00 – I'd like to see you here then too. 9.10 or 9.15 is not good enough.'	Brian confronts Sam directly, saying 'Look, it's not fair you turning up when you feel like it. We can't pick teams, we waste a lot of time, and if you don't turn up we lose the booking at the sports centre.'
Removal of privileges When Tom still fails to get into work on time she sends him a memo telling him that because of his poor timekeeping, his flexitime privileges have been removed, and he may no longer save up extra periods worked to take a day off.	Sam continues to let the bowlers down, so they decide that they'll plan their teams without him, and that if he hasn't arrived within five minutes of the booked time they'll start without him. If he comes late, he can't play.
Suspension and expulsion Maria finally decides she's had enough of Tom. His tardiness is unfair on the others, who are all working a few hours longer each week, just by being on time. She also sees his refusal to improve as a direct challenge to her authority. She gives him a written warning to improve his timekeeping or face the sack, and later fires him.	Sam continues to be erratic putting everyone on edge – arguing with him about whether he can play or not is disruptive. Finally, Brian tells Sam he's not welcome any more, as he's spoiling everyone else's game. Sam blames Brian personally for this expulsion, and is rude and unco-operative when they have to deal with each other at work – the informal group problems have spread into the formal group.

167

The atmosphere is all important – if there is lots of competition between team members, people will be less and less likely to be open about their problems or to admit to mistakes, and at the same time will be less likely to offer help to others. If there's a feeling that some people are getting more rewards (either financial or in terms of praise or recognition) than they deserve, an atmosphere of jealousy may develop. Such emotions are expressed in constant snide remarks, little tricks to undermine the person perceived as 'more favoured', causing stress and tension through the team, reducing performance, both in terms of productivity and quality. This scenario potentially gives rise to all the negative symptoms of stress, such as increased staff illness and absenteeism, malicious gossip, arguments about work issues and a diminution in creativity and optimism.

Like minds and like spirits

As hinted at the previous section, as well as clear communication, working towards common goals, and other practical routes through to good teamwork (aspects that I would label as 'achieving like minds'), I believe that team member exchanges of information about their emotions involving a spiritual coming together can lead on towards excellence in teamwork, and I call this 'achieving like spirits'.

Achieving like minds is really relatively easy. A good example was provided by cabinet government in the Thatcher era. As far as cabinet colleagues were concerned, Margaret Thatcher's economic and political thoughts and perspectives – her mind-set – were what you had to subscribe to and agree with in order to remain on the team. But the moment you ceased having those same thoughts and perspectives, the relationship was fractured instantly and your were off the team. So if the links binding a team together are based on a mind-set – and only on a mind-set – the members' relationships to each other tend to be rather rigid, brittle and easily broken.

If the team is like-spirited as well as like-minded, its structure tends to be much more solid, stable and enduring. We find this with, for example, some family businesses, which enjoy a number of advantages over their non-family counterparts: among other things, they have a more stable culture, greater commitment, more flexibility, and they think in a more long-term way. This is because they are like-spirited as well as like-minded.

So I believe that securing agreement on the spirit of a team is an essential component in ensuring the effectiveness and success of that team. (Indeed, the same applies for whole organisations in relation to the way spirit can be encapsulated in corporate culture, considered later in this chapter.)

Teams that are like spirited develop as a result of the willingness of their members to enter into an exchange of emotional information leading to a mutual discovery of what makes each person tick. This emotional information I call 'core truths', which are the honestly expressed needs, desires and innermost requirements of each of the team members, leading on to the discovery of where they might have common ground. The principle involved here is that 'your pain becomes my pain', and vice versa.

> **Everything comes down to relationships, and there is nowhere we can go to escape them.**

Action

Think about the group of people you would define as your 'team' at work. (Remember that you may be part of more than one team, and although you and a few other people may be common to one or more teams, the teams themselves are quite separate.) Taking each group separately, rate the 'quality of life' within the team on each of the aspects listed in Table 9.2, using the scale on the right, as 'True', 'Sometimes true' and 'Not true'. If the statement is always fully applicable to your team, mark it 'True'. If it's not fully applicable, or not all of the time, mark 'Sometimes true'. If you could rarely or never say that the statement is applicable to your team mark it 'Not true'.

Now, look back over your ticked boxes. If your team is running well, you should have mostly marked 'True' or 'Sometimes True' against the statements. If you've marked many 'Not True' boxes, then you really need to look at the running of your team in those areas.

169

TEAM LEADERS – WHO SHOULD THEY BE?

To be a successful team leader you must have some leadership elements in your personality. You must be organised and balanced, but a certain degree of charisma and likeability is also helpful. The ability to pick up 'vibes' from within or outside the team makes you both better able to help prevent internal team conflict and to help your team cope with changes in the overall organisation or the outside world. The best leaders show consistency and lead by example, providing a stable secure environment for the team to work in.

So, using Human Technology, who makes a good team leader? Different elements of team leadership can be shared among several

Table 9.2

Statement	True	Sometimes true	Not true
Team members feel open and comfortable about expressing doubts and reservations.	☐	☐	☐
We often have discussions in which people express differing views.	☐	☐	☐
We can discuss different opinions without having an argument.	☐	☐	☐
Team members are willing to drop personal hobby-horses in order to achieve a compromise we can all work with.	☐	☐	☐
People don't keep their ideas to themselves, they pass them out to everyone.	☐	☐	☐
If someone is stuck or swamped, another team member will always come to their aid.	☐	☐	☐
We make good use of the skills of everyone in the team.	☐	☐	☐
Individual team members will happily pass on their expertise to new team members or those who are less skilled.	☐	☐	☐
We all know what we're supposed to be doing – both as a team, and as individual members of the team.	☐	☐	☐
Everyone is willing to try out new ideas, new ways of doing things.	☐	☐	☐
Individual team members find it easy to socialise with each other – it's no hardship having to make a train journey in each other's company or sit next to each other at a formal dinner.	☐	☐	☐
We know quite a lot about each other's lives outside work – family, hobbies, lifestyle.	☐	☐	☐

Table 9.2 continued

Statement	True	Sometimes true	Not true
I know the other team members are loyal, and don't do underhand things which destabilise the team.	☐	☐	☐
There's more of a feeling of co-operation than of competition amongst team members.	☐	☐	☐
Everyone accepts responsibility for their own work.	☐	☐	☐
People are willing to do things not strictly within their 'job description' to help the team get the job done.	☐	☐	☐

people – so for example if the 'official leader' is predominantly a Performer, he may choose to rely heavily on a General or Soldier to provide organisation and structure. Remember too, the 'formal' and 'informal' teams which can exist side by side – each of these will commonly have their own leaders. Often leaders of 'informal teams' are people who are broadly Performers, as they are less likely to be given formal authority, but have the drive for leadership as well as the creativity and likeability that tend to attract followers and supporters. If the leaders of the formal and informal teams can learn to recognise and respect one another, they have the opportunity to build a really strong team, with many 'human assets'.

171

The manager's role

Managers are people who get their work done through (not *by*) others. In a very broad sense, the manager's role is as an enabler. He or she is meant to give the people they manage everything they need in order to do the job properly. Some key managerial tasks include:

T foster honest and open communication between team members and between team members and the manager herself;

T set targets for the team and for individuals within the team, making sure that they are clearly understood and accepted;

T treat team members as complex individuals, with lives outside the workplace, learning about what they like and dislike, what they find satisfying and rewarding;

T promote harmony and a pleasant atmosphere within the team – make it a team people want to belong to;

T make sure people are not left out;

T give team members positive feedback, so that they know when they have done something well – identify what's good about their performance;

T encourage people to reach their personal 'peak' of achievement by helping them to try new jobs, take up training, take on extra responsibilities;

T don't dump work on people, but aim to delegate responsibilities with the corresponding sense of achievement and recognition that goes with them;

T think about (and act as representative of your team on) matters of salary, conditions, training, equipment and so on, so that if team members need things in order to perform their jobs properly, you help to get them;

T publicise the achievements of your team and of individuals on it to wider corporate levels – never take sole credit yourself for team successes based on individual or group efforts.

172

The term 'responsibility' featured a number of times in this listing. Remember:

> **Responsibility is responding to our ability, not somebody else's.**

SKILL REQUIREMENTS TO MOVE UP THE CORPORATE LADDER

Figure 9.1 gives you an idea of what's needed to move up from the starting point in the corporate hierarchy, all the way to the top rung. To move up through the first 80 per cent of management, you need important, well-developed technical skills – skills that exemplify the subject matter of the business; so stockbroking, law, soap powder manufacture, and so on. But to get into the top 20 per cent – the management level – you need a completely different set of skills. These are interpersonal, or people skills, involving knowing how to get the best out of people, a willingness to have a team rather than a personal agenda, ambassadorial aptitude, and so on. The more developed these interpersonal skills become, the better team leader you are – and the larger and more influential the team you are allocated to lead.

HOW GOOD IS A TEAM LEADER?

Different sorts of teams, fulfilling different sorts of roles, need different sorts of leader. A deeply analytical, thoughtful manager would be wrong for a team needing quick response, innovation and

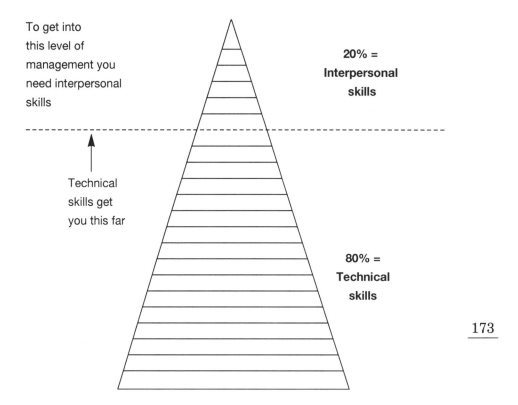

To get into this level of management you need interpersonal skills

20% = Interpersonal skills

Technical skills get you this far

80% = Technical skills

Fig. 9.1 Skill requirements to move up the corporate ladder

flexibility. Someone with a firework personality would be disastrous in a team needing a sensitive or diplomatic approach to difficult subjects or people.

Action

Table 9.3 contains a list of statements about a team leader, which you can use to get a profile of your own team leader. If you are a team leader, you could either ask your team to do it (a measure of your own confidence in your leadership ability would be how you felt about their responses, and whether they felt able to tell you the truth). This is not a 'questionnaire' to be scored – more a checklist of points to think about and discuss. Unlike the earlier 'How good is your team?' list on pages 170–171, it is not necessary to try and get a 'True' rating for every one of these statements. If a team leader knows that he or she is not particularly strong in one management role, then it could be delegated to someone else. This is a sensible solution to the problem that not all human beings can be all things to all men!

Table 9.3

Statement	True	Sometimes true	Not true
Our team leader (TL) is always clear on questions about rules and regulations	☐	☐	☐
I trust my TL's integrity	☐	☐	☐
Our TL is willing to take decisions personally – he/she is not a buck-passer	☐	☐	☐
Everyone on the team shows support for, and solidarity behind, the TL	☐	☐	☐
The TL often asks for comments and discussion on team performance	☐	☐	☐
The TL is always open to suggestions and new ideas	☐	☐	☐
I feel happy about taking problems to the TL	☐	☐	☐
The TL always manages to keep the atmosphere calm, and avoids panic	☐	☐	☐
I've never seen the TL lose his/her temper	☐	☐	☐
Our TL is good at setting goals and deadlines – we always know what we're supposed to be doing	☐	☐	☐
Our TL is fair	☐	☐	☐
I've never seen or heard the TL make personal attacks	☐	☐	☐
If the TL has to criticise an individual for poor performance, or breaking company rules, it's done in private	☐	☐	☐
Our TL is keen on training for all team members	☐	☐	☐

Table 9.3 continued

Statement	True	Sometimes true	Not true
Our TL is a good ambassador from us to the rest of the company, and to the outside world	☐	☐	☐
The TL helps members to learn new skills, and encourages skills exchange	☐	☐	☐
The TL is systematic and thorough	☐	☐	☐
The TL is creative and innovative	☐	☐	☐
The TL is consistent in his/her approach to management	☐	☐	☐
Our TL is flexible about goals and systems in the light of new or changed circumstances	☐	☐	☐
The TL reviews progress towards goals on a regular basis	☐	☐	☐
I can talk to my TL about personal problems	☐	☐	☐
At times of difficulty, our TL always feels reassuringly able to cope	☐	☐	☐
The TL is willing to spend time explaining difficult ideas or concepts, and is willing to pass on his/her skills and expertise to juniors	☐	☐	☐
Our TL is a good problem solver	☐	☐	☐
Our TL shows enthusiasm for our work, and is good at transferring that feeling to other team members	☐	☐	☐

175

Grouping and challenging people in proactive ways

The starting point when building a team is to be very clear about what you want the team to do. Is it supposed to be a hot-house for new ideas? Is it supposed to be a planning group, setting up new systems? Is it supposed to generate sales? Or is it supposed to act as support or implement existing systems efficiently?

When the role of the team is clear, it will be obvious from all we've talked about in this book so far what sort of people you need to make up the team. If you're looking for a team which is intended to run a system carefully and thoroughly, you do not need a team of Performers – even one Performer could be one too many, as he is unlikely to be happy with letting things continue as initially set up, and content himself with getting on with the job. It's much more likely that he would come up with some completely different way of doing things, or be constantly abandoning the daily routine for the more interesting opportunities he sees elsewhere.

But if your team is to be creative, dynamic and innovative, at least one person who is predominantly a Performer will help keep everyone on their toes. As always, the key is clear, truthful communication. If you know you are setting up a team containing several 'leadership' types (Performers and Generals) you need to be very clear about what you expect from them. They need to understand this themselves, and also to know that their own targets are not necessarily the same as those of other team members. So, for example, if you were setting up a team like the Chalkcheese think-tank and actually *selecting* the team members to investigate the installation of new computer systems, (instead of the random selection we saw at the beginning of the book) you might say to yourself:

> 'We need a General in charge of this, someone who can analyse requirements, appoint consultants, compare specifications and quotations and present a structured plan to the board for consideration. But he or she will need some support – there's going to be lots of work compiling documents and figures, ideal for a Soldier. The desirability of some input on emotional problems associated with changes in working practices, and people being reorganised might well mean that a Nurse should be in on all the discussions. Then, we want to take this opportunity to try out really new ideas, not just the most obvious, logical ones that arise from our current systems and ways of doing things. So we should include a Performer in the team.'

As you can see, the think-tank composition could end up being exactly the same as the random selection we started with! But the big difference is that if the reasoning above is followed through, all the members of the think-tank should start out with a clear idea of *why* they've been asked to serve on the team, and what their own roles and responsibilities are. Even more importantly, they know what to expect of the others. So they may not ask Patrick the Performer to turn up to the kinds of sessions where they plan questionnaires and analyse results, but only bring him in when the findings have been boiled down to a final summary.

REORGANISING FOR IMPROVEMENT

Not all teams are started from scratch as happened at Chalkcheese Ltd. Sometimes they already exist, officially or unofficially, and you need to make alterations to the structure, running or leadership of the team in order to make it work better.

If this is your brief, you always need to start from the question, 'What is this team for?' Then you need to ask yourself *why* you feel the team is not performing as well as you expected. Is it that members simply don't have the necessary skills to do the job? Is the team too small, or too overloaded with other work? Or is it some form of 'Human Technology' breakdown? Look back at the statements on the 'How good is your team' list on pages 170–171. They give you an idea of some of the ways in which the human factors within a team can be in conflict, and some of the points you might have to resolve in order to improve the running of the team.

177

When deciding how to improve the team's working, you should consider:

- Improving the team leader's 'interpersonal skills' by training so that he or she understands the workings of the team more thoroughly, and handles the Human Technology elements of the team as well as the commercial nuts and bolts.

- Increasing the skills base of the team by bringing in new members.

- Adding a catalyst to the team in the form of an 'ideas person', with the remit to make suggestions about changes in working practices, targets and systems.

- Utilising the untapped potential of team members by off-loading some of their other work and/or giving them additional training.

- Selecting people from within the team for more challenging roles, or allowing them to take on greater responsibilities.

- Giving rewards and recognition to people in crucial support roles, who may otherwise be disgruntled by the apparent inequity between their positions and those of more high-profile team members.

- Initiating regular round-table meetings at which all members of the team take the opportunity to discuss the team's work openly, encouraging all members to talk about their ideas, problems, errors and worries.

- Taking out of the team any seriously disruptive people – not necessarily sacking them, it may simply be that they are deeply unhappy in the role they play within that particular team, and that their skills and abilities will be better used elsewhere, while the hole they leave behind can be filled by someone happy to play that part.

Goals and agendas

A company's goals can be divided into a hierarchy of:

- corporate
- department (or team)
- individual.

In addition, each of the individuals will have his or her own personal goals. Muddled or poorly understood goals are frustrating for everyone concerned in a company and can result in a great deal of fruitless effort and wasted opportunities.

Agendas refer to the means by which goals are to be realised, and may include timetables or deadlines. For example, a food processing company might set as an overall corporate goal:

to consolidate and maintain the company's market share in the face of increasing competition from new players in the marketplace following the reduction in trade barriers.

It helps when setting goals to set some form of measurability, so that it's possible to tell whether and when targets have been met or exceeded. The company might want to measure its performance in terms of turnover, market share or profitability, and to record on what basis the measurements are to be taken.

The agenda set for achieving this overall goal might include a number of sub-goals, which are usually more specific than the overall goal, such as:

to increase brand awareness and customer loyalty to the company's products;

to develop new products to compete with new types of imports.

Each sub-goal carries its own agenda, timetable and basis for measurement of achievement of targets. Department or team goals should be set, so that each group knows the targets it is expected to meet in order to help the company achieve the overall goals, such as:

Market research: to collect data on (a) customer perceptions of current products – what is liked/disliked, how they see the products compared to other products in terms of quality, price, value for money, packaging, etc, and (b) what new products are now being imported into the country and how they are being received by the home market.

The market research department will certainly split these tasks down into smaller, more manageable units, and different teams will be assigned to separate tasks such as questionnaire design, selecting sample populations, compiling data on new products through trade literature, and so on.

At the team and individual levels, the number of goals tend to proliferate, and they also become more firmly defined, with a fixed timetable. Deadlines are more likely to be set as particular days, or even times, rather than over a period of years. Achievement of each goal should aid the overall development towards the achievement of the corporate goal. So the sales force might be given the additional objective of selling a range of new products to retailers, but in order to meet the overall objective of 'consolidating and maintaining the company's market share', they must also continue to actively sell the traditional product lines, and not allow orders for these to fall away.

179

WORKING OUT CLASHES BETWEEN TEAM AND PERSONAL GOALS

A Human Technology problem that reveals itself when corporate and team goals and agendas are set, is that such goals and agendas can conflict with the personal goals and agendas of the individuals who have to try and meet them. These clashes must be resolved if the team (and the company) are to succeed and thrive. The individual must feel that his or her goals are best served by striving to fulfil the team and corporate goals. Table 9.4 shows how individuals and teams tend to conflict.

FLEXIBILITY AND CHANGES TO GOALS

Goal setting at all levels must allow flexibility and revisions to goals – changes in technology, opportunities for new developments and acquisitions, legal and regulatory changes might all force companies to rethink both goals and strategies. Changes in personnel, equipment and workload might mean a department or team has to rethink its plans, while personal circumstances affect the way an individual reconciles his or her personal and 'work' goals.

Table 9.4

Individual	Team
• Personal agenda	• Group agenda
• Private goals	• Group goals
• Covert – political atmosphere	• Overt
• Avoids risks	• Thrives on challenges
• Compete against each other	• Compete together against external opponents
• Non-co-operative, defensive	• Mutually supportive
• No real communication	• Communicate intensively
• Puts up with, suffers mistakes, misses opportunities	• Outperforms itself
• Needs to be kick-started	• Internally motivatved

The major point to remember here is that if your goals are graven in stone, you could be carving your headstone!

Corporate rhythm and culture

It's usually obvious what the principal goals or targets of a business are – they could be defined in terms of turnover, profits, market penetration, or whatever, but generally people know and understand *what* they are. Therefore, goals and targets are usually not mysterious, but what is often mysterious is the pace and rhythm that the team adopts in working together in order to achieve the corporate goals.

An analogy I use is that of a team of six rowers who, one lunchtime, decide to row their boat across a harbour from their boathouse on one shore to a pub on the opposite shore – so, as a team, the pub is their goal. Now it only takes one oarsman out of the six to be rowing at a different rhythm to all the rest, and the boat will end up going round in circles. A common rhythm or rate of achievement is essential if the boat crew is to reach their goal.

It's an interesting aspect that the other people on the boat may be unaware of the effect the one oarsman who is out of sync is having on the group's success. Once the course has been set and they all begin rowing they may well not realise that the crab-catcher is taking them off course. It's only observers on the shore who, seeing the erratic progress of the boat, will deduce that there is something going wrong – that instead of a smooth progress across the harbour the boat is going round in huge circles. As far as the crew is concerned, spending hours rowing very hard trying to get to the pub, they are likely to end up exhausted without having gone anywhere, and frustrated by not knowing why all their hard work has not got them anywhere. Even the odd-man-out may not know that his different rhythm is what has caused the problem.

I think this analogy helps us to home in on the hugely important point that, in any team activity, it is crucial to set goals and specify targets, but it's the rhythm adopted in undertaking tasks in order to achieve the goals that is often the key.

COMPANY CULTURE

Every organisation, whatever the size, has a definable culture, philosophy or corporate personality. To present a homogeneous and stable image, each component of the company must know, support and implement the corporate culture. Many companies fail to clarify a desirable culture and the consequent multi-interpretations present a confused image to customers or clients. Culture friction is often the dominant issue in the successful implementation of a merger or acquisition.

This can be very hard for newcomers to take on board. Someone who has come from an organisation where things were done with great care and thoroughness, with many levels of checking and rechecking, will be horrified if they move into another operation with a more 'have-a-go' attitude. Their colleagues, used to working at speed, taking decisions without consultations and putting up with a certain level of errors in order to achieve low-cost targets or tight deadlines, may complain of the newcomer as slow, ponderous and pedantic. The newcomer is in a very difficult position. First of all she may doubt her own abilities – everyone else seems to be getting so much more done than she is, and she just doesn't know if she can work that way. Secondly, there's a dichotomy. Has she perhaps been hired *because* of her thoroughness and care? Is she meant to try and bring in the kind of quality control systems, the checking and double checking that resulted in higher quality work that she was used to before?

Defining the company culture, explaining it to newcomers, and changing it where necessary is a major role of the team leader. He or she must recognise how the company ticks, and help newcomers to fit in.

Indeed, sometimes I am called in by companies to help them clarify and define what their corporate culture should be. Here are three examples from recent assignments:

---

1 After many hours of discussion and analysis, the chairman of a public relations company felt that the key buzz words (the 'essence') of his organisation ought to be 'class, clout and consistency'. He wanted people to perceive the organisation as classy – acting for high-powered, prestigious clients; as having clout – with ready access to key media figures and opinion-formers; and as consistently delivering the class and the clout.

2 At a large environmental services company I found the firm almost entirely staffed by an extremely highly qualified (PhDs etc), multidisciplined workforce. They were predominantly left-brain people and tended to wait for work to come to them, but this was not happening in the recession. So I spent some time with the board and it was decided they needed to adopt a new culture, and this involved the acronym PAID – 'Pushy, Ambitious, Initiative, Deliver' – in many ways the antithesis of the cloistered, academic, almost isolationist culture that had grown up.

3 A medium-sized bank in one of the American states was worried about the attitude of disinterest displayed to customers by many of its tellers. The US banking market is highly competitive, and the directors felt the quality of people fronting its operations was not up to the standards that had to be achieved. Previously, the main emphasis had been placed on operating effectively in the overall US market. The board, realising this was all irrelevant if they couldn't perform the basic task of keeping local customers happy, demoted interstate aspirations to third place in their redefinition of the bank's corporate culture – 'to be anxious to please, to be supportive, and to be a major player'.

I often think that clarifying and defining the company culture represents the most important ingredient of success – it is absolutely essential. In *all* of these examples, what happened afterwards was that it immediately became clear that many senior people in the organisation did not fit in at all with the newly defined corporate culture, that some new people should be recruited who would reflect the new atmosphere and be able to enthuse others, and that some existing staff should be moved to other jobs or departments within the organisation in which their particular personality and talents would mean they could better project the new culture.

The different Human Technology types will find difficulties fitting into particular company cultures. For example, if someone who is predominantly a Performer were suddenly hired into an organisation in which all decisions were taken after elaborate discussion, where actions were strongly rooted in tradition, and where all the staff were accustomed to structure and regulation, he might quickly find himself at odds with his new colleagues. This is not to say you can never import a Performer into a structured organisation of this type, but that the consequent real problems must be considered, and the organisation must be ready to respond flexibly.

Action

The list of statements in Table 9.5 reflect company culture and rhythm, both of which are linked to management style. As before, check off 'True', 'Sometimes True' or 'Not True' against each statement, to help you compile a picture of the culture within your organisation.

TIMING

In the ebb and flow of any group activity, some people are more important at certain times than others. If a football team is under attack from the opposition, its defenders are the most important team members, but if the ball is cleared upfield, the team's strikers become much more important to team success. Similarly in business organisations, in times of recession the people who are predominantly Generals are more important; there is little need for Performer salesmen at that time because there is nobody to sell to. However, the others should make clear to the Performer that this situation is OK with them and that they understand his position. They know he would like to be zipping around, seeing a lot of people, networking and selling, but he should not feel guilty if the circumstances dictate that he treads water for a while.

ERROR MANAGEMENT

> **There is great value in mistakes. We only really learn from getting it wrong, because this is when we find out what doesn't work.**

A good gauge of company culture is how the organisation deals with mistakes. If the usual reaction to the discovery of an error is to start a witch-hunt, laying all the blame for the mistake on a single person, who is then punished for it, then no one is going to be willing to draw attention to errors if they don't have to. The other unhelpful attitude is that of the 'noble leader': 'It's my department, it's my mistake.' Well, fine, but if that's as far as it goes, and no effort is made to discover the true cause of the error and prevent it from recurring, then the 'noble manager' might as well fall on his sword straight away for all the good he's doing.

Mistakes are important. They usually mean that some part of the system is not functioning properly, and tracking down their cause can lead to the discovery of hidden insecurities, frustration, or grey areas of responsibilities which have persisted and caused waste and disruption for a long time, without leading to an actual 'error'.

Table 9.5

Statement	True	Sometimes true	Not true
Everyone here takes a pride in theiir work, and in the company	☐	☐	☐
I feel I know the managers – they're part of the 'team' too	☐	☐	☐
We often re-evaluate traditional systems	☐	☐	☐
The managers like to feel that everyone is happy in their work	☐	☐	☐
When I'm trying to achieve something, I feel that others in the company are with me, not against me	☐	☐	☐
The company is doing its best to keep up with a rapidly changing world	☐	☐	☐
People are encouraged to develop their lives outside work – not to spend too much extra time in the office	☐	☐	☐
Managers are objective when judging people – no one is rewarded because 'their face fits'	☐	☐	☐
Top management keep in touch with day-to-day operations	☐	☐	☐
We never feel 'in the dark' about company information	☐	☐	☐
When things are difficult or busy, we all pull together	☐	☐	☐
Creativity and new ideas are welcomed and rewarded by management	☐	☐	☐
I feel I get a fair reward for my input – I don't feel exploited	☐	☐	☐
People tend to stay on with the company	☐	☐	☐

Table 9.5 continued

Statement	True	Sometimes true	Not true
Staff are flexible and willing to try out new ideas	☐	☐	☐
You don't have to be a 'yes-person' to succeed here	☐	☐	☐
Assessment standards and procedures are clear	☐	☐	☐
Staff feel comfortable about expressing opinions to each other and management	☐	☐	☐
We can take advantage of modern technology and methods	☐	☐	☐
People at all levels can accept positive criticism	☐	☐	☐
Individual and team goals are clearly defined	☐	☐	☐
You never see people losing their tempers or having rows	☐	☐	☐
We don't have anyone who 'coasts'	☐	☐	☐
I know what my responsibilities are	☐	☐	☐
We've got access to all the skills and technical knowledge we need – either in-house or available outside	☐	☐	☐
There's an atmosphere of enthusiasm about the job	☐	☐	☐
My ideas always get a hearing – even if they are a bit 'off the wall'	☐	☐	☐
Teams and departments have good communications links	☐	☐	☐
Teams and departments co-operate with each other rather than competing	☐	☐	☐
Planning meetings look to the future, as well as at progress on current projects	☐	☐	☐

185

Table 9.5 continued

Statement	True	Sometimes true	Not true
We have a good error management system	☐	☐	☐
Everyone takes on responsibilities – not just managers	☐	☐	☐
Time is set aside for training	☐	☐	☐
We always look at problems as teams or departments, and try and find solutions	☐	☐	☐
No one worries about being made a scapegoat	☐	☐	☐
Management trusts us to work unsupervised	☐	☐	☐
There are opportunities for promotion from within	☐	☐	☐

Errors should always be tackled by teams, not by individuals – including managers. Team communication and cohesiveness must be such that individuals feel able to bring mistakes to the attention of the team, its leader and to other managers. This means also that the individuals within the team need to have confidence in themselves, and to know that their own self-image won't be irretrievably damaged by admitting to a mistake.

The first step is to try and minimise the damage caused by the mistake, and this is where the team is so valuable. A group of people acting as 'fire-fighters' – redoing a job, trying to catch up on schedules, soothing irritated clients, can almost always do a better job than someone acting alone. If outsiders such as customers or other departments go away with a negative impression of your team's ability to deliver, based on an error, they may never come back to give you another chance. If an error has been made, your best chance is to make sure they go away thinking 'Well, you have to hand it to them – even if they get it wrong, they move heaven and earth to put it right, and I bet it'll never happen again!'

Next establish the cause of the error – which bit of the system is not working. Then the team should set up, or improve the existing system to prevent the same sort of error recurring. For example, more help might be needed for overworked staff, additional training if staff skills fall short of what's needed, or additional layers of checking and quality control for complex work.

Fostering teams – motivation, incentives and rewards

In business, the main reward is often seen as financial. But this is really a 'secondary' reward – money is no use in itself, it's useful for the things it can buy, and the way our work is structured we tend to receive the same amount of money whether we give 100 per cent or 80 per cent of our abilities. If we drop to 50 per cent of our abilities, we do stand a chance of getting fired, or at least of not receiving promotion (and the higher pay that goes with it) or even the regular pay rises that others get (if the company operates a flexible pay system).

Performance-related pay, profit shares, bonuses, and so on, all help to relate financial reward to work done. But there are pluses as well as minuses here. On the minus side, it can be very difficult to quantify some people's contributions, and to assess their correct levels of reward – who deserves the bonus, for example, the sales director who has persuaded a new client to bring a major contract to the firm, or her efficient secretary, without whom she might not have had all the background on the firm, got to the meeting on time, followed up with letters and proposals as promised and remembered to call at regular intervals until the deal was closed. Support people have a major role in the running of all companies, and need to be recognised and rewarded.

Another minus point about performance-related pay particularly, is that we all need a certain level of security. We need to know that our mortgage is covered, we can pay the essential bills, we can afford the supermarket shop on the weekend. If too much of our income is variable, and based on results, this can be destabilising and frightening. This is particularly so when market conditions make it increasingly difficult to perform successfully.

For rewards to act as incentives, there are various things to remember:

- For a reward to work, it must be seen as worthwhile by the recipient – if a teacher praises a child publicly for good work, the child may be embarrassed at being ' Teacher's pet'.
- The bigger the gap between the reward and the behaviour being rewarded, the less likely it is that the recipient will connect the two.
- If a reward is expected for certain behaviour, and not received, gradually the behaviour will stop – 'Why bother doing extra work,

187

taking extra care, bringing in new clients, if nobody notices or cares?'

■ Rewards must vary depending on what you've done to deserve them. If you work really hard, giving 100 per cent, and the person next to you does much less, giving 80 per cent, and you both receive the same level of praise for a job well done, or the same performance-related bonus, then next time you won't bother to put in as much effort – or you'll consider going somewhere else where your efforts are more appreciated.

PUNISHMENT

Strict regulations, sanctions for disobeying these, and the constant threat of losing one's job if targets are not met are the least effective means of motivating staff. The carrot and the pat are much more successful than the stick. In a company where people are given little flexibility and responsibility there's no incentive for them to give more than minimally necessary to get the job done, and a positive disincentive to 'stick one's head above the parapet'. Punishing someone for incorrect behaviour in no way tells them what the appropriate or preferred behaviour is, so gives them no clues about how they are supposed to behave.

Of course, in a commercial context, there have to be rules, and there have to be disciplinary measures when these are flouted. But in a good team, with a good team leader, these can be largely replaced by the rewards of the team's success and culture. Timekeeping, for example, becomes less of a problem when everyone in the team realises that their poor timekeeping can impact negatively on the other team members, and that it's unfair if some team members are working longer hours than others, when you all have the same goals in view. If responsibilities are distributed amongst team members, then the team as a whole will express disapproval of individuals who don't pull their weight, changing the focus from 'manager versus staff member' to 'team against team member'.

TRAINING AND BRIEFING

As we've seen throughout this chapter, good training and clear briefings are crucial to the success of teams. No one can do their job properly if not given the skills to do it with. Skills can be a combination of formal technical skills and 'local knowledge' which should be passed on by managers and other team members. In poorly functioning teams and organisations with a corporate culture of 'every man for himself' there can be a tendency to keep 'local knowledge' to oneself. This is a combination of the feeling, 'If I'm the only one who knows how to do this, then my job is always secure' and, 'I had to get this knowledge the hard way, why shouldn't everyone else?'

Knowledge is power, but instead of seeing it as an exclusive source of power, the successful team should view group knowledge as more empowering than any individual's knowledge.

Briefing – telling people what's going on, what the goals are, what's expected of them – should be clear and frequent. It may be necessary to constantly change and refine goals and targets, and it's important that people understand that the changes are taking place, and know that they have to adjust their focus appropriately.

ASSESSMENT

Employees and team members should be encouraged to keep a record of what they do, which should be discussed openly when rewards or punishments are handed out. That way it will be clear to them what the reward is for, helping them to identify the kinds of work practice likely to get rewards in the future.

189

Team members should know in advance what they will be assessed on, but assessments should take place immediately if serious problems are occurring – waiting three months until the next scheduled session means far too much water will have flowed under the bridge. Team members should also be made aware of how the assessment will be done and what its implications will be. Moving the goalposts is not fair on the individual, and is unproductive, creating an atmosphere of unease and insecurity.

Assessment *must* take place however. Team members should see it as a positive feature of their work, helping them to get feedback on how to improve their performance, and to know when they have fulfilled expectations and met targets.

Chalkcheese Ltd – the epilogue

The think-tank members have been informed of the board's decision to install system B, and have been formally thanked for their efforts in preparing the report and recommendations. To their surprise (and some dismay), they've also been asked to continue to act as liaison with Cliff Thompson, the computer consultant, and the individual department managers as the system is installed, and people are retrained – a matter of months or even years, rather than weeks! Can they work together without problems for that length of time? They decide to celebrate the end of the first stage, by going out to lunch together, and also to discuss how to proceed in the future.

Natalie: How nice this is! We should have sat down and got to know each other a bit before we started the think-tank meetings.

Stuart: Yes, indeed. For instance, I hadn't realised just how long you've been with the company – nor had I realised how well you understand the way all the different departments work. I tend to see something of their finances, but I really know very little about their day-to-day activities.

Gail: So, what about the next stage? I suppose we all thought we'd be finished when the report went in.

Patrick: Surely we can leave most of it to the computer experts, like Cliff?

Natalie: I don't think anyone sees us as 'managing' the new installation in any way – but after all, we know more about it than anyone else within Chalkcheese. Perhaps our role is just to help 'sell' the idea to all the staff and managers.

Gail: And to calm their fears – people will be worried that they won't be able to cope with the new technology, or that they'll be replaced by a machine!

Stuart: How should we go about it?

Gail: Well, Patrick is the best of all of us at 'selling' – when you talk about the new systems, you get really excited, and it all sounds like fun. I think you should be the 'front-person' for the think-tank.

190

Patrick: Yes, OK, that's a good idea – I can make encouraging speeches at the drop of a hat!

Stuart: Right! What about Natalie working with Patrick – she knows so many people in different parts of the company, and everyone likes her. You'd be good at getting people to talk about any worries they may have.

Natalie: Well, if you're sure – but I'm not sure I can explain things to people!

Gail: Don't worry. We can make a list of the most common queries and worries from the work we've already done when we questionnaired the departments before preparing the report. With that in hand, you should be able to answer 90 per cent of the questions. And anything too technical, you can refer to the consultants.

Stuart: What about you and I?

Gail: Since the system's going to be installed piece-by-piece, I think we should concentrate on making a detailed implementation plan with the department managers, and the computer people. Then we'll have to track operations – and costs – carefully, because the board is going to expect regular updates and progress reports.

Patrick: This all sounds great! Everyone is going to do things that they're good at, and enjoy! I think we'll make a great team!

CREATING EFFECTIVE TEAMS – A CHECKLIST

■ Teams at work should integrate individuals, providing a support system and 'family' to belong to.

■ Both formal and informal teams play a role in the smooth running of the organisation and can help to establish and uphold the company culture and rhythm.

■ Open, honest, multiway communication is essential for an effective team. Each team member, including leaders, must feel able, and have the opportunity to express opinions, suggest new ideas, air grievances and ask for help with problems.

■ Managers are people who get their work done through (not by) people. Managers (team leaders) are enablers – they give people everything they need to do their work effectively and in a rewarding way.

■ If your team is made up of 'support' people only, you are unlikely to see many new initiatives arising spontaneously from it's members. If it consists entirely of leadership types, it may suffer from the 'too many chiefs and not enough indians' syndrome.

191

■ Goal setting should be done at corporate levels, department or team levels, and individual levels. One role of team leaders is to help team members realise personal goals through workplace goals.

■ Motivating teams and individuals should take place through a combination of rewards, incentives and punishments, but the use of punishments and sanctions should be kept to a minimum.

10

Curing conflict

Preventing and resolving conflict is the ultimate goal. If conflict can be cured in yourself and others, you will go a long way towards generating a more fulfilled productive team with benefits for all. This chapter draws together the main themes of the book to help ensure that consensus is created and conflict stays cured.

Conflict is waste

192   Throughout this book we've seen how conflict and friction cause waste:

- waste of time
- waste of money
- waste of energy
- waste of emotion
- waste of resources
- waste of people.

Waste of people is the biggest waste of all – they are the most valuable 'equipment' an organisation can have.

An important conclusion in Chapter 1 ('Facing up to friction') was that the pretence that conflict is not happening, or the refusal to accept the signs of friction and impending conflict are as damaging and wasteful as conflict itself. Opening up about the problems, giving them some air, is the first step to blowing them away completely. Learn to recognise:

- signs of *friction within yourself*, including:
  - irritation
  - resentment
  - fear
  - stress
  - a sense of ill-being (as opposed to well-being)
  - insecurity
  - self-doubt
  - apathy

- depression
- anger
- jealousy

■ signs of *friction in others*, such as:
  - anger
  - snide remarks
  - undermining
  - withholding information
  - unwillingness to share
  - reluctance to co-operate
  - defensive attitude
  - lack of humour
  - frequent ill health
  - irritability
  - a refusal to change
  - low enthusiasm

■ signs of *friction within the company*, for example:
  - poor interdepartmental communication
  - slow decision making
  - mistakes and poor quality work
  - drops in productivity
  - clock-watching
  - senior managers unfamiliar with staff
  - poor attendance at meetings
  - no open discussion of complaints
  - new ideas not followed up
  - absenteeism;
  - frequent use of company's disciplinary procedures.

193

The first step is to recognise that there is a problem. The next step is to do something about it. However, be aware of the 'last straw' conflict – the problem which has been brewing for a long time, but where the participants have decided:

'Oh, I won't bother to say anything about it this time because:'

■ it's not a good moment
■ he's probably under a lot of stress
■ I haven't got time to deal with it
■ she's in a terrible mood
■ too many other people are listening
■ it seems rather trivial.

The day will come when something happens that is regarded as 'the last straw', and suddenly a whole mass of pent-up irritation or resentment will come pouring out. Usually the recipient of this torrent is completely taken aback by the violence of the response to what seems to him or her to be a fairly minor transgression. When they realise they are expected to answer for a whole catalogue of sins they had long ago forgotten, they usually become defensive and angry, and a conflict situation springs fully-blown from (apparently) nothing at all.

Conflict within people

The conflict within, is the first and most important conflict to resolve. If you are confident, happy, and secure about your abilities, role and achievements, then the slings and arrows of daily life leave you relatively unscathed.

Thinking about yourself and your reactions helps you achieve the greatest form of knowledge – self-knowledge, leading to:

- self-awareness
- self-acceptance
- self-belief
- self-confidence
- self-esteem
- self-respect
- self-love.

We examined some of the underlying reasons why people behave as they do in Chapter 2 ('Understanding what makes people tick'), and, throughout the book, other factors affecting how we feel about ourselves have been highlighted. Let's review some of these, using them as indicators of internal conflict.

CENTRING

Centred people have achieved a balance between all the forces trying to push them in different directions, and they feel comfortable with themselves. Becoming, and remaining, centred should be a major goal of our lives. Figure 10.1 gives a schematic idea of the uncentred emotions, pressures and constraints on the periphery of our existence, and the core 'centred' position we should strive for.

We need to question our actions and feelings constantly:

> 'Why did I refuse to help my colleague? Was I really too busy? Or was I afraid that he would use my help to take away some of my expertise, to get ahead of me? Am I acting from the uncentred emotion of jealousy and insecurity?'

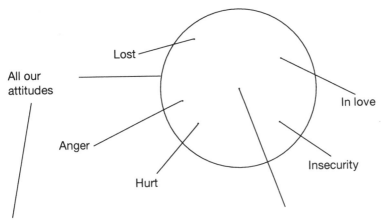

In an 'attitude'
Tense
Off balance
Distressed
Uncommitted
Unreliable
Purposeless
Irresponsible
Dishonest
Little integrity
Uncomfortable to be around
Closed to input
Have to be right
Closed to change
Makes poor decisions
Gives less than 100 per cent
Emotional/Problem causing

All of the above produces:

MEDIOCRITY

Feeling centred
Tranquil
Balanced
Calm
Committed
Reliable
Purposeful
Responsible
Honest
Peace of mind
Comfortable to be around
Open to input
Able to be wrong
Open to change
Makes good decisions
Gives 100 per cent
Factual/Problem solving

All of the above produced:

EXCELLENCE

195

Fig. 10.1 Attitudes, behaviour and centring

'Why did I snap at my children when I arrived home from work? Were they really making so much mess and noise? Or am I feeling guilty because I'm not there to play with them during the day? Do I feel guilty because I really want to play with them, or because somewhere in me is the rule 'Mothers should give their children 100 per cent'?'

'I felt really good about myself today! What caused that? What did I do or say that really satisfied and pleased me? Can I repeat that, and help myself to retain this feeling of contentment and reward?'

Don't accept the status quo of your own emotions. Be open to change and discoveries. Identify what makes you happy or sad, satisfied or angry, irritated or pleased. An uncentred person – a person suffering internal conflict – is wasting his or her life, and is performing far below optimum.

> **If we are only open to discoveries that accord with what we already know, then we might as well stay closed.**

Becoming centred

Moving towards centring means taking control and refusing to be the victim, and the key idea in achieving a centred existence involves recognising and acknowledging the core truths about your needs, desires and emotional requirements. Centred people have the opportunity to achieve excellence, while uncentred people can only achieve mediocrity. Figure 10.2 gives you some ideas about moves you have to make for yourself in order to take control, and achieve centring.

ACCEPTING CHANGE

We talked about change in Chapter 6, and looked at the principal stages or levels in the process of change:

- *Spiritual:* the germ of an idea that change is possible.
- *Intellectual:* the plan of an idea plus logical reasons why change is desirable.
- *Emotional:* the uneasy or anxious feelings that change is necessary.
- *Physical:* the body's indication that change is overdue.

The time to change is during the spiritual and emotional stages. At these times it's still possible to face the moves with equanimity and to imagine making the changes effortlessly. Once you've moved into the emotional and physical stages, other aspects of your life are affected. People close to you will be suffering from the conflict you're suppressing within yourself. It gets more and more difficult to identify just what it is that is making you unhappy – what it is you need to do something about. The danger is that you'll avoid the need for change for so long that when the crash eventually comes, you'll make the mistake of throwing away parts of your life that you will later regret losing.

THE ATTITUDE	THE ATTITUDE
• I'm giving 100 per cent to the job in hand. • I've made a total commitment. • I'm honest with myself. • I'm honest with others. • I believe I have integrity. • I am trustworthy. • I take complete responsibility for my actions. • I have faith in myself. • I am prepared to be innovative. • I am self-disciplined. • I'm willing to take a risk, with my own abilities. • I'm prepared to be wrong. • I can fail at something, without destroying myself.	• I do just enough to get by at the job. • I haven't committed myself. • I'm not honest with myself and others. • I lack integrity. • I feel dissatisfied and unfulfilled. • My abilities can only go so far. • I never really know what's going on. • I'm judgemental about myself and others. • I avoid responsibility. • I blame others when things go wrong, and for my problems. • I do things at the wrong time.
leads to **THE REWARD**	**leads to** **THE REWARD**
Fulfilment Creativity Satisfaction Feeling of self-worth Happiness Abundance Power Rejuvenation Health Having friends Purpose	Unhappiness Boredom Lethargy Depression Illness Poor shape Loneliness Lack of balance Feeling lost Dis-stress Vulnerability
leads to **THE END PRODUCT**	**leads to** **THE END PRODUCT**
I feel in control of my life.	I feel like a victim.

197

Fig. 10.2 Feeling in control; or feeling a victim

KNOWING YOURSELF

Throughout this book we've used the idea of the Human Technology system to provide a basis for thinking about people, particularly with regard to their best work roles, and their expectations of, and interactions with, others. To recap, Human Technology helps you to group together certain behavioural characteristics of yourself and other people to give you a broad overall picture of an individual. You then get an idea of how you or that individual will respond in certain situations, what types of activity, including work, will be most rewarding and satisfying, how interactions with other people are likely to proceed and so on.

Chapter 3 and 4 discussed the Human Technology system in detail, and suggested some ways of identifying the different types. The characteristics of the four types are summarised in Figure 10.3.

	Performers	Generals	Soldiers	Nurses
Typical characteristics	visionary intuitive charismatic creative independent illogical spontaneous unstructured bad listener emotional needs change	organised team leader goal-oriented structured logical factual authoritative academic responsible good listener needs consistency	loyal supportive team player solid unimaginative consistent thick-skinned traditional patient thorough boring	emotional caring creative defensive considerate mothering vulnerable prickly supportive moody instinctive
Core traits ↓	leader passionate instinctive	leader logical problem-solving	supporter methodical unwavering	supporter emotional caring
Ideal jobs ↓	entrepreneur sales/marketing public relations	accounting lawyer company director	manual worker line manager loyal employee	nurse teacher secretary
Corporate role ↓	ideas generator networker expansion/change	good provider planner problem-solver	supporter goal implementer	supporter goal implementer

Fig. 10.3 A summary of the four Human Technology types

198

Thinking about your Human Technology type can help you to understand why you run into certain sorts of conflict again and again throughout all parts of your life. For example, someone who is predominantly a Nurse may look back on her life and see a history of emotional upsets with people she cares about. Well, if you are that Nurse, remember that you make very heavy emotional demands on people, and that your need for love and affection may be higher than other types. It's very difficult for them to live up to your needs, or to know what is expected of them. What you've seen as rejection, disloyalty or betrayal in someone you cared for may never have been intended as such by them. On the other hand, your need for love may have frightened or overwhelmed them with emotional demands they found hard to cope with or understand.

> **Everything that is unresolved in previous relationships will turn up in your present ones.**

Someone whose primary component is Performer may have to accept that he is no good at planning or following through with detailed implementation. But having recognised and accepted these aspects of himself, the sensible Performer will surround himself with people who *are* good at both aspects. He will also have to discipline himself to communicate with the people in those roles, and to listen to their advice, but without compromising the 'edge' that he has over others – his vision and creativity, and enthusiasm for new ideas.

When using the Human Technology system it is important to remember that *no one* is 100 per cent of any one type. We all have a primary and a secondary component, and the ratio of primary to secondary differs from person to person.

199

Learning to identify your secondary component is as important as identifying your primary component. Your secondary component may give you what your primary component lacks. So a Performer-Soldier, even one who is predominantly (say 70 per cent) Performer, will gain some 'stick-at-it-ness' from his Soldier side, giving some stability and follow-through to the normally Will-o'-the-wisp Performer.

Performers and Nurses are right brain – instinctive, creative, and emotional. Soldiers and Generals are left brain – logical and problem solving. Usually (although not always), your primary component comes from one side of the brain, and your secondary component from the other. So, even if your primary component is very dominant, you have the ability and the opportunity to access characteristics and attributes from the other side of your brain.

LIFESPAN CHANGE

Another point that we looked at in Chapters 3 and 4 is the way that your Human Technology type develops with age. On achieving adulthood, people mainly rely on their secondary component to help them 'sort life out', solve problems and make decisions, and this secondary component continues as the main driving force until around about age 35 to 42 (although generally later for Soldier personalities). At this point, people 'move into' and feel more at ease with their primary component. This often appears as taking control of your circumstances and feeling empowered, rather than letting someone else make important decisions for you.

However, this shift can be a major cause of painful change in mid-life. Like the changes of puberty, but without the obvious physical aspects, people are concerned to find themselves behaving differently, wanting different things, losing job satisfaction, getting pleasure from different sources, feeling different emotions. They resist these changes, thinking 'Why should I suddenly throw away everything I've worked for, just for a whim?' This major life change is no whim.

To illustrate, a General-Nurse at this life point, and working in an office environment has, up to now, taken a supportive role, happy to help others get ahead, sort out problems and grateful for their liking and thanks in return. Now, she's more likely to want some recognition and reward for her organising ability, to take on more responsibility, to be in charge. Her reaction might be to seek promotion, or to consider going into business for herself.

200

Conflict between people

This section considers expectations, communication and power.

EXPECTATIONS

One problem is that we all have expectations of each other. We expect managers to be organised, secretaries to be supportive, and directors to be decisive. (See Chapter 5 for a discussion of expectations and roles.) We generally pay very little attention to the real characteristics of the individuals in these roles. It's as though we expect a person to put on a whole new set of behavioural characteristics, like putting on a coat, when they enter a particular role. It's like outstanding salesmen who get promoted to management, only to fall flat.

One way to defuse and prevent conflict between people is to make it clear what their roles are. Remember too, that people may play several roles. For example, a salesperson who travels to visit customers might take the roles of 'company representative', 'deal-maker' and 'negotiator' while on the road, then come back to the office to take up the role of 'feedback conduit', providing the office-bound personnel with information about how their work, products or services are being received by the outside world. Conflict will certainly arise if the salesperson is not filling those roles adequately – if for instance he never bothers to pass back comments about problems or inquiries from customers to the office, and concentrates solely on making sales.

Another way to prevent conflict is to consider the personality types of the people filling the roles. Sending a Nurse out to fulfil the salesperson's role above would clearly be a mistake. A Nurse would not have the thick skin required to take the knocks and rebuffs that commonly befall sales people, and would probably lack the organising ability to analyse and feed back customer information to the office in a structured and useful way.

COMMUNICATION

> **If the people you are communicating with do not get the message, you have failed, not them. Take responsibility for the communication.**

We've talked about communication, and the importance of telling the truth, throughout this book, but particularly in Chapter 6 ('Influencing reactions in others'). At its simplest level, if you want someone to do something, or to stop doing something, you have to tell them so.

201

Just to summarise, here are a few 'rules' for successful communication:

- Communication should be two- (or multi-) way. Lectures and speeches are not the same thing.
- Listening is a key part of communication – as important as speaking.
- Communications should be tailored to the person (or people) you're communicating with. Avoid being patronising or obscure, over-simplifying or over-complicating.
- Communicating with Soldiers, Performers, Nurses and Generals each requires a distinctive approach.
- Make sure you start from common ground – you should all be talking and thinking about the same thing.
- Be direct, not oblique. Don't hint.
- Avoid incomplete communications.
- Choose an appropriate venue.
- Don't mix emotion and fact.
- All comments on others' performance, whether praise or criticism, should be positive. There is no point in telling people they've done something badly, if you don't tell them how to do it better.

- Don't make assumptions. (Remember about the word **assume**: assumptions make an **ass** out of **u** and **me**).

- If you think more is meant than is being said, ask questions and use feedback.

- Don't ignore possible hints – make people come out in the open.

- Don't 'read between the lines'. You should not have to interpret.

- Your opinions and values, likes and dislikes, feelings and concerns are yours – don't project them on to others. They have their own approach to the world, and it may not match yours.

- Avoid prejudging a conversation or scenario. Wait and see what transpires before you practise your reaction to it.

- Brevity is less likely to be boring!

POWER

Power, the struggle to acquire it, and the misuse of it is the major source of conflict. But ironically, it's those *with* power who have the best chance of resolving conflict. We looked at the nature of power, power games, and the difference between power and authority, in Chapter 7. Then again in Chapter 9 we saw how the power of a well-integrated, mutually supportive team can be vastly greater than the power of any single individual within that team. The struggle for power can be seen in all sorts of situations – we start to try and gain power as children, when our parents and teachers seem to have all the control, and we have none. We vie for power in our family and social relationships – someone can almost always be labelled as 'dominant' in every situation.

The drive to acquire power varies in the different Human Technology types. Generals are the most likely to want to take control, to build armies of loyal supporters and to dictate to others. But we all want a certain level of power over our own lives. Someone who is constantly at the mercy of the whims and dictates of others will feel very little control. This leads to low self-esteem, a lowering of optimism, symptoms of stress and a movement away from centring. Power games in a corporate setting damage the company, the players and all who get caught up in the struggle.

Here again, good communication is the best defence. Anyone caught up in a power struggle must make their position and feelings clear, and avoid taking sides. Sharing your problems with others in the same position empowers you all, bonding together to prevent the warring factions from trampling you underfoot one by one.

Conflict in organisations

This book has focused on conflict within the organisational and corporate settings, looking at the tensions within people when they are unhappy or insecure in their work role, and between people who come into conflict as a result of organisational/corporate proximity or competition. But there are also group-group conflicts – disputes between employers and staff, for example, or between rival businesses.

GOALS AND ASPIRATIONS

In Chapter 9 we talked about companies that are bad at setting clear, overall corporate goals, and at translating those into sub-goals, departmental goals and individual targets. This gives rise to grey areas, in which no one is quite sure what is wanted, or what the aims are. People work hard at the wrong things, and are penalised, then feel unfairly treated. Motivation and morale drop – there's a sense of aimlessness, of lack of purpose.

Communication is again the key – asking: 'What are my targets?' 'Is there a way you'd prefer me to get there?' 'How does this link with the targets of others?' 'What are the end-goals, and how do my goals lead towards them?' will help to prevent conflict from developing.

Personal goals may also be in conflict with corporate goals. For example, someone whose ambition and drive leads them to want to innovate and change things will be in direct conflict with the corporate goals of a company that is trying to consolidate and batten down the hatches. If the members of a team are concentrating on competing with each other, instead of co-operating to compete with the outside, then the personal ambitions of the members can prevent the team achieving its goals.

Preventing such clashes from hindering a company's progress is the job of the managers in the company. At the most senior level, goal setting is one of the major responsibilities of the board of directors. Goals should never be left vague, but should be fully described, and should include some kind of measurability, as well as a time-scale. These goals should also be translated into a working strategy, including sub-goals and targets for individuals, teams, and departments. Again, these must be clear, and measurable. It's then the job of individual team leaders to discuss these openly with team members. The leader must make sure that the team member:

- is the right type of person to undertake the task of achieving the goal
- understands the goal
- accepts the goal – ie, is willing to put conflicting personal goals aside

and concentrate on achieving the team goal

- has the skills, time and support to achieve the goal.

An interesting recent development in the United States has extended the ideas of corporate goals to encompass formally drafted 'aspiration statements' – not just what the company's people want to do, but how they want to be. The board of jeans maker Levi Strauss, for example, attributes a significant part of the company's recent financial recovery to a huge increase in employee morale following adoption of its aspiration statement. The flavour is apparent from one passage that reads:

> 'We want our people to feel respected, treated fairly, listened to, and involved. Above all we want satisfaction from accomplishments and friendships, balanced personal and professional lives, and to have fun in our endeavours.'

Chief executive Bob Haas is fond of emphasising the theme by frequent reminders to employees along the lines: 'You don't work *for* Levi's, you work for yourselves; you just happen to work *at* Levi's.'

CORPORATE CULTURE AND RHYTHM

A common cause of conflict within companies, also discussed in Chapter 9, is differences in corporate culture and rhythm. It's particularly noticeable when, for example, mergers between companies take place, and two groups of employees, used to different cultures, have to try and work harmoniously. New managers and staff members, coming in from other companies, may also find that although they do their work adequately, they don't seem to 'fit in', no-one seems to appreciate what they're doing.

Feeling productive and being proud of one's contribution is the basis for raising morale.

Clashes of corporate culture and rhythm are much harder to identify and remedy than those caused by inadequately defined corporate goals, or even clashes between personal and corporate goals. That's because these elements are 'unwritten'. No one makes a *rule* saying, 'in this company, when there's a flap on, everyone works through lunch and stays late until the crisis is over, even if timekeeping is relaxed at other times.' But the newcomer who packs up at 12.30 to go off to lunch when everyone else is tearing their hair out, trying to finish a project before 4.00, will get dirty looks at the least from his colleagues, and behind his back people will question his loyalty and commitment to the team.

Managers have the best chance of sorting out such clashes, first, by being aware that this rather vague area can give rise to problems, and second by communicating directly about it. If the team manager realises that the deadline means that for a day or so everyone will have to put 'all hands to the pump', then he should announce this, to everyone concerned. It should be expressed in the form of a goal:

> *'Our team really needs to complete this project by 4.00pm on Friday. If we go past that time, it will be too late to catch the courier to head office, and won't arrive in time for the decision on Monday. I know that it's going to be really difficult to do it in the time, but I'd like you all to put aside other work for the moment, and concentrate on this. Those of you who are not directly concerned with the project can help those who are by fielding phone calls about other work, maybe taking on some of the non-specialist tasks like assembling and copying documents. If we all pull together, we can do it. People who put in extra time, over lunch, or in the evenings, please keep a note, and we can arrange time off in lieu.'*

NEGOTIATION

We looked at negotiation in Chapter 8, in the context of deadlock – the situation where opposing parties are in open conflict, and refuse to give up on a position or demands. Actually, negotiation goes on at every level, all the time: 'If I wash the dishes, will you take the rubbish out?' is a common domestic bargain for example. In the 'urgent project' described in the previous section, the team leader is negotiating for staff to put in extra hours with the offer of time off in lieu as a bargaining counter.

The first thing to remember in negotiation is that there is no point in trying to negotiate in a situation where there is no common ground. All the parties in a negotiation must have a mutual interest, and this must not be lost sight of in the attempt to gain what each side wants. For example a salesman and a customer both want the sale to be completed – the salesman wants to get the highest possible price and the customer wants the lowest possible price. But if they don't agree on a price, the deal falls through, and both lose.

The target in negotiations is to get to a situation where no party feels it has 'lost'. In the most successful negotiations, all parties go away satisfied that they have 'won'. Winning is not necessarily doing the other party down, getting something from them or gaining ascendancy over them. Winning is not even necessarily getting what you want. It could be finding a solution that none of the parties thought of when the dispute started, or finding one that can be seen as a move forward – a step which allows negotiation to proceed.

Last word

No conflict situation is unrecoverable. Conflict can always be prevented, and can always be cured. The main message of this book is that *conflict is all about people*, and I believe that people – provided they are willing to take responsibility for their lives – are amazingly flexible, resilient, and open to change. That's why they are the most valuable resource a company can have, and their well-being is synonymous with the well-being of the business. The growth in business comes from the growth in people.

Index

■